Ethnic Groups and Boundaries

The Social Organization of Culture Difference

Edited by
FREDRIK BARTH

WAVELAND

PRESS, INC.

Long Grove, Illinois

For information about this book, contact:
Waveland Press, Inc.
4180 IL Route 83, Suite 101
Long Grove, IL 60047-9580
(847) 634-0081
info@waveland.com
www.waveland.com

Contents

Preface 1998

The reprinting of this collection of essays should not be seized as an opportunity to rethink and rewrite its contents: there is already a vast and continuing literature doing just that. Instead, in view of the influence that the volume still has, I will simply point to a few of its central ideas so the contemporary reader may read the text more easily. My colleagues and I were, after all, engaging in a debate with our contemporaries of thirty years ago, not with you; and it is useful to be clear about to whom the text speaks.

Most anthropologists at the time thought, at least implicitly, that the world could be described usefully as a discontinuous array of entities called societies, each with its internally shared culture, and that this framed the issues of ethnicity. They further assumed that each such entity should be analysed in a structural-functional paradigm to display its systematic order and functional integration.

Our argument against that view is still important, because similar ways of thinking are constantly being reintroduced into the social science literature, deriving either from the commonsense reifications of people's own discourse and experience or from the rhetoric of ethnic activists. It is true that the word "ethnic" is used to refer to groups of people who are considered to have a shared identity, a common history, and a traditional cultural heritage. But these features may not in themselves provide the best bases for analysing and understanding ethnic phenomena. The breakthrough we were striving for during our symposium in 1967 was to identify the particular processes whereby ethnic groups are formed and made relevant in social life. To do so, we were looking for something like mechanisms, not for descriptions of manifest forms. We were trying to see social organization as emergent and contested, culture as something characterized by variation and flux, and to think of cases of relative stability in ethnic and other social relations as being as much in need of explanation as cases of change.

These were largely counter-intuitive positions judged by the assumptions that prevailed at the time. They represented, perhaps, one of the first anthropological applications of a more postmodern view of culture. Though we lacked the opaque language of present-day postmodernism, we certainly argued for what would now be recognized as a constructionist view. Likewise in our view of history, we broke loose from the idea of history as simply the objective source and cause of ethnicity and approached it as a form of synchronic rhetoric—a struggle to appropriate the past, as one might say today.

To achieve our breakthrough, our empirical strategy was to give particular ethnographic attention to the anomalous persons who *change* their ethnic identity: a discovery procedure aiming to lay bare the processes involved in the reproduction of ethnic groups. The most heterodox and still contentious sentence in my Introduction is the most central: I urge us to focus the investigation on "the ethnic *boundary* that defines the group, not the cultural stuff that it encloses" (p. 15). This highlights our emphases:

- that ethnicity is a matter of social organization above and beyond questions of empirical cultural differences: it is about "the social organization of culture difference";
- that ethnic identity is a matter of self-ascription and ascription by others in interaction, not the analyst's construct on the basis of his or her construction of a group's "culture";
- that the cultural features of greatest import are boundary-connected: the diacritica by which membership is signalled and the cultural standards that actors themselves use to evaluate and judge the actions of ethnic co-members, implying that they see themselves as "playing the same game."

Of course, these are perforce "cultural" matters, as much as is the "cultural stuff" I urged the analyst *not* to focus on. The point is, they are the cultural materials that the actors themselves are deploying to construct their own identities and actions, they are not whatever cultural materials the analyst might wish to bring in to characterize cultural differences that may persist between the two populations. To assess this analytical recipe properly, readers should combine the Introduction with the substantive essays, both my own and the others, as many critics have failed to do.

In somewhat similar fashion, when looking at ethnic conflict we sought to refocus on the meta-level of ethnic leadership, asking how conflicts may be manipulated to strengthen leadership positions, not merely what cultural issues are substantively addressed in the discourse. Likewise, in analysing indigenous people's political activism, we discussed the shift to seeing such groups as engaged in a social struggle for meaningful change, not the revitalization of an unchanging heritage of aboriginal cultural traits.

These and many other issues are still important and urgent, perhaps even increasingly so, in our contemporary world. It is my hope that the reprinting of these essays will play a positive role in helping to provide the best possible foundations for a searching analysis and debate on the many enduring and emerging issues of ethnicity today.

Introduction

by Fredrik Barth

This collection of essays addresses itself to the problems of ethnic groups and their persistence. This is a theme of great, but neglected, importance to social anthropology. Practically all anthropological reasoning rests on the premise that cultural variation is discontinuous: that there are aggregates of people who essentially share a common culture, and interconnected differences that distinguish each such discrete culture from all others. Since culture is nothing but a way to describe human behaviour, it would follow that there are discrete groups of people, i.e. ethnic units, to correspond to each culture. The differences between cultures, and their historic boundaries and connections, have been given much attention; the constitution of ethnic groups, and the nature of the boundaries between them, have not been correspondingly investigated. Social anthropologists have largely avoided these problems by using a highly abstracted concept of 'society' to represent the encompassing social system within which smaller, concrete groups and units may be analysed. But this leaves untouched the empirical characteristics and boundaries of ethnic groups, and the important theoretical issues which an investigation of them raises.

Though the naïve assumption that each tribe and people has maintained its culture through a bellicose ignorance of its neighbours is no longer entertained, the simplistic view that geographical and social isolation have been the critical factors in sustaining cultural diversity persists. An empirical investigation of the character of ethnic boundaries, as documented in the following essays, produces two discoveries which are hardly unexpected, but which demonstrate the inadequacy of this view. First, it is clear that boundaries persist despite a flow of personnel across them. In other words, categorical ethnic distinctions do not depend on an absence of mobility, contact and information, but do entail social processes of exclusion and incorporation whereby discrete categories are maintained *despite* changing participation and membership in the course of individual life histories. Secondly, one finds that stable, persisting, and often vitally important social relations are maintained across such boundaries, and are frequently based precisely on the dichotomized ethnic statuses. In other words, ethnic distinctions do not depend on an absence of social interaction and acceptance, but are quite to the contrary often the very foundations on which embracing social systems are built. Interaction in such a social system does not lead to its liquidation through change and acculturation; cultural differences can persist despite inter-ethnic contact and interdependence.

General approach

There is clearly an important field here in need of rethinking. What is required is a combined theoretical and empirical attack: we need to investigate closely the empirical facts of a variety of cases, and fit our concepts to these empirical facts so that they elucidate them as simply and adequately as possible, and allow us to explore their implications. In the following essays, each author takes up a case with which he is intimately familiar from his own fieldwork, and tries to apply a common set of concepts to its analysis. The main theoretical departure consists of several interconnected parts. First, we give primary emphasis to the fact that ethnic groups are categories of ascription and identification by the actors themselves, and thus have the characteristic of organizing interaction between people. We attempt to relate other characteristics of ethnic groups to this primary feature. Second, the essays all apply a generative viewpoint to the analysis: rather than working through a typology of forms of ethnic groups and relations, we attempt to explore the different processes that seem to be involved in generating and maintaining ethnic groups. Third, to observe these processes we shift the focus of investigation from internal constitution and history of separate groups to ethnic boundaries and boundary maintenance. Each of these points needs some elaboration.

Ethnic group defined

The term ethnic group is generally understood in anthropological literature (cf. e.g. Narroll 1964) to designate a population which:
1. is largely biologically self-perpetuating

2. shares fundamental cultural values, realized in overt unity in cultural forms

3. makes up a field of communication and interaction

4. has a membership which identifies itself, and is identified by others, as constituting a category distinguishable from other categories of the same order.

This ideal type definition is not so far removed in content from the traditional proposition that a race = a culture = a language and that a society = a unit which rejects or discriminates against others. Yet, in its modified form it is close enough to many empirical ethnographic situations, at least as they appear and have been reported, so that this meaning continues to serve the purposes of most anthropologists. My quarrel is not so much with the substance of these characteristics, though as I shall show we can profit from a certain change of emphasis; my main objection is that such a formulation prevents us from understanding the phenomenon of ethnic groups and their place in human society and culture. This is because it begs all the critical questions: while purporting to give an ideal type model of a recurring empirical form, it implies a preconceived view of what are the significant factors in the genesis, structure, and function of such groups.

Most critically, it allows us to assume that boundary maintenance is unproblematical and follows from the isolation which the itemized characteristics imply: racial difference, cultural difference, social separation and language barriers, spontaneous and organized enmity. This also limits the range of factors that we use to explain cultural diversity: we are led to imagine each group developing its cultural and social form in relative isolation, mainly in response to local ecologic factors, through a history of adaptation by invention and selective borrowing. This history has produced a world of separate peoples, each with their culture and each organized in a society which can legitimately be isolated for description as an island to itself.

Ethnic groups as culture-bearing units

Rather than discussing the adequacy of this version of culture history for other than pelagic islands, let us look at some of the logical flaws in the viewpoint. Among the characteristics listed above, the sharing of a common culture is generally given central importance. In my view, much can be gained by regarding this very important feature as an implication or result, rather than a primary and definitional characteristic of ethnic group organization. If one chooses to regard the culture-bearing aspect of ethnic groups as their primary characteristic, this has far-reaching implications. One is led to identify and distinguish ethnic groups by the morphological characteristics of the cultures of which they are the bearers. This entails a prejudged viewpoint both on (1) the nature of continuity in time of such units, and (2) the locus of the factors which determine the form of the units.

1. Given the emphasis on the culture-bearing aspect, the classification of persons and local groups as members of an ethnic group must depend on their exhibiting the particular traits of the culture. This is something that can be judged objectively by the ethnographic observer, in the culture-area tradition, regardless of the categories and prejudices of the actors. Differences between groups become differences in trait inventories; the attention is drawn to the analysis of cultures, not of ethnic organization. The dynamic relationship between groups will then be depicted in acculturation studies of the kind that have been attracting decreasing interest in anthropology, though their theoretical inadequacies have never been seriously discussed. Since the historical provenance of any assemblage of culture traits is diverse, the viewpoint also gives scope for an 'ethnohistory' which chronicles cultural accretion and change, and seeks to explain why certain items were borrowed. However, what is the unit whose continuity in time is depicted in such studies? Paradoxically, it must include cultures in the past which would clearly be excluded in the present because of differences in form — differences of precisely the kind that are diagnostic in synchronic differentiation of ethnic units. The interconnection between 'ethnic group' and 'culture' is certainly not clarified through this confusion.

2. The overt cultural forms which can be itemized as traits exhibit the effects of ecology. By this I do not mean to refer to the fact that they reflect a history of adaptation to environment; in a more immediate way they also reflect the external circumstances to which actors must accommodate themselves. The same group of people, with unchanged values and ideas, would surely pursue different patterns of life and institutionalize different forms of behaviour when faced with the different opportunities offered in different environments? Likewise, we must expect to find that one ethnic group, spread over a territory with varying ecologic circumstances, will exhibit regional diversities of overt institutionalized behaviour which do not reflect differences in cultural orientation. How should they then be classified if overt institutional forms are diagnostic? A case in point is the

distributions and diversity of Pathan local social systems, discussed below (pp. 117 ff.). By basic Pathan values, a Southern Pathan from the homogeneous, lineage-organized mountain areas, can only find the behaviour of Pathans in Swat so different from, and reprehensible in terms of, their own values that they declare their northern brothers 'no longer Pathan'. Indeed, by 'objective' criteria, their overt pattern of organization seems much closer to that of Panjabis. But I found it possible, by explaining the circumstances in the north, to make Southern Pathans agree that these were indeed Pathans too, and grudgingly to admit that under those circumstances they might indeed themselves act in the same way. It is thus inadequate to regard overt institutional forms as constituting the cultural features which at any time distinguish an ethnic group — these overt forms are determined by ecology as well as by transmitted culture. Nor can it be claimed that every such diversification within a group represents a first step in the direction of subdivision and multiplication of units. We have well-known documented cases of one ethnic group, also at a relatively simple level of economic organization, occupying several different ecologic niches and yet retaining basic cultural and ethnic unity over long periods (cf., e.g., inland and coastal Chuckchee (Bogoras 1904-9) or reindeer, river, and coast Lapps (Gjessing, 1954).

In one of the following essays, Blom (pp. 74 ff.) argues cogently on this point with reference to central Norwegian mountain farmers. He shows how their participation and self-evaluation in terms of general Norwegian values secures them continued membership in the larger ethnic group, despite the highly characteristic and deviant patterns of activity which the local ecology imposes on them. To analyse such cases, we need a viewpoint that does not confuse the effects of ecologic circumstances on behaviour with those of cultural tradition, but which makes it possible to separate these factors and investigate the non-ecological cultural and social components creating diversity.

Ethnic groups as an organizational type
By concentrating on what is *socially* effective, ethnic groups are seen as a form of social organization. The critical feature then becomes item (4) in the list on p. 11 the characteristic of self-ascription and ascription by others. A categorical ascription is an ethnic ascription when it classifies a person in terms of his basic, most general identity, presumptively determined by his origin and background. To the extent that actors use ethnic identities to categorize themselves and others for

purposes of interaction, they form ethnic groups in this organizational sense.

It is important to recognize that although ethnic categories take cultural differences into account, we can assume no simple one-to-one relationship between ethnic units and cultural similarities and differences. The features that are taken into account are not the sum of 'objective' differences, but only those which the actors themselves regard as significant. Not only do ecologic variations mark and exaggerate differences; some cultural features are used by the actors as signals and emblems of differences, others are ignored, and in some relationships radical differences are played down and denied. The cultural contents of ethnic dichotomies would seem analytically to be of two orders: (i) overt signals or signs — the diacritical features that people look for and exhibit to show identity, often such features as dress, language, house-form, or general style of life, and (ii) basic value orientations: the standards of morality and excellence by which performance is judged. Since belonging to an ethnic category implies being a certain kind of person, having that basic identity, it also implies a claim to be judged, and to judge oneself, by those standards that are relevant to that identity. Neither of these kinds of cultural 'contents' follows from a descriptive list of cultural features or cultural differences; one cannot predict from first principles which features will be emphasized and made organizationally relevant by the actors. In other words, ethnic categories provide an organizational vessel that may be given varying amounts and forms of content in different socio-cultural systems. They may be of great relevance to behaviour, but they need not be; they may pervade all social life, or they may be relevant only in limited sectors of activity. There is thus an obvious scope for ethnographic and comparative descriptions of different forms of ethnic organization.

The emphasis on ascription as the critical feature of ethnic groups also solves the two conceptual difficulties that were discussed above.

1. When defined as an ascriptive and exclusive group, the nature of continuity of ethnic units is clear: it depends on the maintenance of a boundary. The cultural features that signal the boundary may change, and the cultural characteristics of the members may likewise be transformed, indeed, even the organizational form of the group may change — yet the fact of continuing dichotomization between members and outsiders allows us to specify the nature of continuity, and investigate the changing cultural form and content.

2. Socially relevant factors alone become diagnostic for membership, not the overt, 'objective' differences which are generated by other factors. It makes no difference how dissimilar members may be in their overt behaviour — if they say they are A, in contrast to another cognate category B, they are willing to be treated and let their own behaviour be interpreted and judged as A's and not as B's; in other words, they declare their allegiance to the shared culture of A's. The effects of this, as compared to other factors influencing actual behaviour, can then be made the object of investigation.

The boundaries of ethnic groups
The critical focus of investigation from this point of view becomes the ethnic *boundary* that defines the group, not the cultural stuff that it encloses. The boundaries to which we must give our attention are of course social boundaries, though they may have territorial counterparts. If a group maintains its identity when members interact with others, this entails criteria for determining membership and ways of signalling membership and exclusion. Ethnic groups are not merely or necessarily based on the occupation of exclusive territories; and the different ways in which they are maintained, not only by a once-and-for-all recruitment but by continual expression and validation, need to be analysed.

What is more, the ethnic boundary canalizes social life — it entails a frequently quite complex organization of behaviour and social relations. The identification of another person as a fellow member of an ethnic group implies a sharing of criteria for evaluation and judgement. It thus entails the assumption that the two are fundamentally 'playing the same game', and this means that there is between them a potential for diversification and expansion of their social relationship to cover eventually all different sectors and domains of activity. On the other hand, a dichotomization of others as strangers, as members of another ethnic group, implies a recognition of limitations on shared understandings, differences in criteria for judgement of value and performance, and a restriction of interaction to sectors of assumed common understanding and mutual interest.

This makes it possible to understand one final form of boundary maintenance whereby cultural units and boundaries persist. Entailed in ethnic boundary maintenance are also situations of social contact between persons of different cultures: ethnic groups only persist as significant units if they imply marked difference in behaviour, i.e.

persisting cultural differences. Yet where persons of different culture interact, one would expect these differences to be reduced, since interaction both requires and generates a congruence of codes and values — in other words, a similarity or community of culture (cf. Barth 1966, for my argumentation on this point). Thus the persistence of ethnic groups in contact implies not only criteria and signals for identification, but also a structuring of interaction which allows the persistence of cultural differences. The organizational feature which, I would argue, must be general for all inter-ethnic relations is a systematic set of rules governing inter-ethnic social encounters. In all organized social life, what can be made relevant to interaction in any particular social situation is prescribed (Goffman 1959). If people agree about these prescriptions, their agreement on codes and values need not extend beyond that which is relevant to the social situations in which they interact. Stable inter-ethnic relations presuppose such a structuring of interaction: a set of prescriptions governing situations of contact, and allowing for articulation in some sectors or domains of activity, and a set of proscriptions on social situations preventing inter-ethnic interaction in other sectors, and thus insulating parts of the cultures from confrontation and modification.

Poly-ethnic social systems

This of course is what Furnivall (1944) so clearly depicted in his analysis of plural society: a poly-ethnic society integrated in the market place, under the control of a state system dominated by one of the groups, but leaving large areas of cultural diversity in the religious and domestic sectors of activity.

What has not been adequately appreciated by later anthropologists is the possible variety of sectors of articulation and separation, and the variety of poly-ethnic systems which this entails. We know of some of the Melanesian trade systems in objects belonging to the high-prestige sphere of the economy, and even some of the etiquette and prescriptions governing the exchange situation and insulating it from other activities. We have information on various traditional poly-centric systems from S.E. Asia (discussed below, Izikowitz pp. 135 ff.) integrated both in the prestige trade sphere and in quasi-feudal political structures. Some regions of S.W. Asia show forms based on a more fully monetized market economy, while political integration is poly-centric in character. There is also the ritual and productive cooperation and political integration of the Indian caste system to be considered, where perhaps only kinship and domestic life remain as a proscribed sector and a wellspring for cultural diversity. Nothing can be gained by lumping these various systems under the increasingly vague label of 'plural' society, whereas an investigation of the varieties of structure can shed a great deal of light on social and cultural forms.

What can be referred to as articulation and separation on the macro-level corresponds to systematic sets of role constraints on the micro-level. Common to all these systems is the principle that ethnic identity implies a series of constraints on the kinds of roles an individual is allowed to play, and the partners he may choose for different kinds of transactions.[1] In other words, regarded as a status, ethnic identity is superordinate to most other statuses, and defines the permissible constellations of statuses, or social personalities, which an individual with that identity may assume. In this respect ethnic identity is similar to sex and rank, in that it constrains the incumbent in all his activities, not only in some defined social situations.[2] One might thus also say that it is *imperative*, in that it cannot be disregarded and temporarily set aside by other definitions of the situation. The constraints on a person's behaviour which spring from his ethnic identity thus tend to be absolute and, in complex poly-ethnic societies, quite comprehensive; and the component moral and social conventions are made further resistant to change by being joined in stereotyped clusters as characteristics of one single identity.

The associations of identities and value standards

The analysis of interactional and organizational features of inter-ethnic relations has suffered from a lack of attention to problems of boundary maintenance. This is perhaps because anthropologists have reasoned from a misleading idea of the prototype inter-ethnic situation. One has tended to think in terms of different peoples, with different histories and cultures, coming together and accommodating themselves to each other, generally in a colonial setting. To visualize the basic requirements for the coexistence of ethnic diversity, I would suggest that we rather ask ourselves what is needed to make ethnic distinctions *emerge* in an area. The organizational requirements are clearly, first, a categorization of population sectors in exclusive and imperative status categories, and second, an acceptance of the principle that standards applied to one such category can be different from that applied to another. Though this alone does not explain why cultural

2. Barth

differences emerge, it does allow us to see how they persist. Each category can then be associated with a separate range of value standards. The greater the differences between these value orientations are, the more constraints on inter-ethnic interaction do they entail: the statuses and situations in the total social system involving behaviour which is discrepant with a person's value orientations must be avoided, since such behaviour on his part will be negatively sanctioned. Moreover, because identities are signalled as well as embraced, new forms of behaviour will tend to be dichotomized: one would expect the role constraints to operate in such a way that persons would be reluctant to act in new ways from a fear that such behaviour might be inappropriate for a person of their identity, and swift to classify forms of activity as associated with one or another cluster of ethnic characteristics. Just as dichotomizations of male versus female work seem to proliferate in some societies, so also the existence of basic ethnic categories would seem to be a factor encouraging the proliferation of cultural differentiae.

In such systems, the sanctions producing adherence to group-specific values are not only exercised by those who share the identity. Again, other imperative statuses afford a parallel: just as both sexes ridicule the male who is feminine, and all classes punish the proletarian who puts on airs, so also can members of all ethnic groups in a poly-ethnic society act to maintain dichotomies and differences. Where social identities are organized and allocated by such principles, there will thus be a tendency towards canalization and standardization of inter-action and the emergence of boundaries which maintain and generate ethnic diversity within larger, encompassing social systems.

Interdependence of ethnic groups

The positive bond that connects several ethnic groups in an encompassing social system depends on the complementarity of the groups with respect to some of their characteristic cultural features. Such complementarity can give rise to interdependence or symbiosis, and constitutes the areas of articulation referred to above; while in the fields where there is no complementarity there can be no basis for organization on ethnic lines — there will either be no interaction, or interaction without reference to ethnic identity.

Social systems differ greatly in the extent to which ethnic identity, as an imperative status, constrains the person in the variety of statuses and roles he may assume. Where the distinguishing values connected with ethnic identity are relevant only to a few kinds of activities, the social organization based on it will be similarly limited. Complex poly-ethnic systems, on the other hand, clearly entail the existence of extensively relevant value differences and multiple constraints on status combinations and social participation. In such systems, the boundary maintaining mechanisms must be highly effective, for the following reasons: (i) the complexity is based on the existence of important, complementary cultural differences; (ii) these differences must be generally standardized within the ethnic group — i.e. the status cluster, or social person, of every member of a group must be highly stereotyped — so that inter-ethnic interaction can be based on ethnic identities; and (iii) the cultural characteristics of each ethnic group must be stable, so that the complementary differences on which the systems rest can persist in the face of close inter-ethnic contact. Where these conditions obtain, ethnic groups can make stable and symbiotic adaptations to each other: other ethnic groups in the region become a part of the natural environment; the sectors of articulation provide areas that can be exploited, while the other sectors of activity of other groups are largely irrelevant from the point of view of members of any one group.

Ecologic perspective

Such interdependences can partly be analysed from the point of view of cultural ecology, and the sectors of activity where other populations with other cultures articulate may be thought of as niches to which the group is adapted. This ecologic interdependence may take several different forms, for which one may construct a rough typology. Where two or more ethnic groups are in contact, their adaptations may entail the following forms:

(1) They may occupy clearly distinct niches in the natural environ-ment and be in minimal competition for resources. In this case their interdependence will be limited despite co-residence in the area, and the articulation will tend to be mainly through trade, and perhaps in a ceremonial-ritual sector.

(2) They may monopolize separate territories, in which case they are in competition for resources and their articulation will involve politics along the border, and possibly other sectors.

(3) They may provide important goods and services for each other, i.e. occupy reciprocal and therefore different niches but in close inter-dependence. If they do not articulate very closely in the political

sector, this entails a classical symbiotic situation and a variety of possible fields of articulation. If they also compete and accommodate through differential monopolization of the means of production, this entails a close political and economic articulation, with open possibilities for other forms of interdependence as well.

These alternatives refer to stable situations. But very commonly, one will also find a fourth main form: where two or more interspersed groups are in fact in at least partial competition within the same niche. With time one would expect one such group to displace the other, or an accommodation involving an increasing complementarity and interdependence to develop.

From the anthropological literature one can doubtless think of type cases for most of these situations. However, if one looks carefully at most empirical cases, one will find fairly mixed situations obtaining, and only quite gross simplifications can reduce them to simple types. I have tried elsewhere (Barth 1964b) to illustrate this for an area of Baluchistan, and expect that it is generally true that an ethnic group, on the different boundaries of its distribution and in its different accommodations, exhibits several of these forms in its relations to other groups.

Demographic perspective

These variables, however, only go part of the way in describing the adaptation of a group. While showing the qualitative, (and ideally quantitative) structure of the niches occupied by a group, one cannot ignore the problems of number and balance in its adaptation. Whenever a population is dependent on its exploitation of a niche in nature, this implies an upper limit on the size it may attain corresponding to the carrying capacity of that niche; and any stable adaptation entails a control on population size. If, on the other hand, two populations are ecologically interdependent, as two ethnic groups in a symbiotic relationship, this means that any variation in the size of one must have important effects on the other. In the analysis of any poly-ethnic system for which we assert any degree of time depth, we must therefore be able to explain the processes whereby the sizes of the interdependent ethnic groups are balanced. The demographic balances involved are thus quite complex, since a group's adaptation to a niche in nature is affected by its *absolute* size, while a group's adaptation to a niche constituted by another ethnic group is affected by its *relative* size.

The demographic problems in an analysis of ethnic inter-relations in a region thus centre on the forms of recruitment to ethnic groups and the question of how, if at all, their rates are sensitive to pressures on the different niches which each group exploits. These factors are highly critical for the stability of any poly-ethnic system, and it might look as if any population change would prove destructive. This does not necessarily seem to follow, as documented e.g. in the essay by Siverts (pp. 101 ff.), but in most situations the poly-ethnic systems we observe do entail quite complex processes of population movement and adjustment. It becomes clear that a number of factors other than human fertility and mortality affect the balance of numbers. From the point of view of any one territory, there are the factors of individual and group movements: emigration that relieves pressure, immigration that maintains one or several co-resident groups as outpost settlements of larger population reservoirs elsewhere. Migration and conquest play an intermittent role in redistributing populations and changing their relations. But the most interesting and often critical role is played by another set of processes that effect changes of the identity of individuals and groups. After all, the human material that is organized in an ethnic group is not immutable, and though the social mechanisms discussed so far tend to maintain dichotomies and boundaries, they do not imply 'stasis' for the human material they organize: boundaries may persist despite what may figuratively be called the 'osmosis' of personnel through them.

This perspective leads to an important clarification of the conditions for complex poly-ethnic systems. Though the emergence and persistence of such systems would seem to depend on a relatively high stability in the cultural features associated with ethnic groups — i.e. a high degree or rigidity in the interactional boundaries — they do *not* imply a similar rigidity in the patterns of recruitment or ascription to ethnic groups: on the contrary, the ethnic inter-relations that we observe frequently entail a variety of processes which effect changes in individual and group identity and modify the other demographic factors that obtain in the situation. Examples of stable and persisting ethnic boundaries that are crossed by a flow of personnel are clearly far more common than the ethnographic literature would lead us to believe. Different processes of such crossing are exemplified in these essays, and the conditions which cause them are shown to be various. We may look briefly at some of them.

Factors in identity change

The Yao described by Kandre (1967b) are one of the many hill peoples on the southern fringe of the Chinese area. The Yao are organized for productive purposes in extended family households, aligned in clans and in villages. Household leadership is very clear, while community and region are autochthonously acephalous, and variously tied to poly-ethnic political domains. Identity and distinctions are expressed in complex ritual idioms, prominently involving ancestor worship. Yet this group shows the drastic incorporation rate of 10 % non-Yao becoming Yao in each generation (Kandre 1967a: 594). Change of membership takes place individually, mostly with children, where it involves purchase of the person by a Yao houseleader, adoption to kinship status, and full ritual assimilation. Occasionally, change of ethnic membership is also achieved by men through uxorilocal marriage; Chinese men are the acceptable parties to such arrangements.

The conditions for this form of assimilation are clearly twofold: first, the presence of cultural mechanisms to implement the incorporation, including ideas of obligations to ancestors, compensation by payment, etc., and secondly, the incentive of obvious advantages to the assimilating household and leader. These have to do with the role of households as productive units and agro-managerial techniques that imply an optimal size of 6–8 working persons, and the pattern of intra-community competition between household leaders in the field of wealth and influence.

Movements across the southern and northern boundaries of the Pathan area (cf. pp. 123 ff.) illustrate quite other forms and conditions. Southern Pathans become Baluch and not vice versa; this transformation can take place with individuals but more readily with whole households or small groups of households; it involves loss of position in the rigid genealogical and territorial segmentary system of Pathans and incorporation through clientage contract into the hierarchical, centralized system of the Baluch. Acceptance in the receiving group is conditional on the ambition and opportunism of Baluch political leaders. On the other hand, Pathans in the north have, after an analogous loss of position in their native system, settled in and often conquered new territories in Kohistan. The effect in due course has been a reclassification of the settling communities among the congeries of locally diverse Kohistani tribes and groups.

Perhaps the most striking case is that from Darfur provided by Haaland (pp. 58 ff.), which shows members of the hoe-agricultural Fur of the Sudan changing their identity to that of nomadic cattle Arabs. This process is conditional on a very specific economic circumstance: the absence of investment opportunities for capital in the village economy of the Fur in contrast to the possibilities among the nomads. Accumulated capital, and the opportunities for its management and increase, provide the incentive for Fur households to abandon their fields and villages and change to the life of the neighbouring Baggara, incidentally also joining one of the loose but nominally centralized Baggara political units if the change has been economically completely successful.

These processes that induce a flow of personnel across ethnic boundaries will of necessity affect the demographic balance between different ethnic groups. Whether they are such that they contribute to stability in this balance is an entirely different question. To do so, they would have to be sensitive to changes in the pressure on ecologic niches in a feed-back pattern. This does not regularly seem to be the case. The assimilation of non-Yao seems further to increase the rate of Yao growth and expansion at the expense of other groups, and can be recognized as one, albeit minor, factor furthering the progressive Sinization process whereby cultural and ethnic diversity has steadily been reduced over vast areas. The rate of assimilation of Pathans by Baluch tribes is no doubt sensitive to population pressure in Pathan areas, but simultaneously sustains an imbalance whereby Baluch tribes spread northward despite higher population pressures in the northern areas. Kohistani assimilation relieves population pressure in Pathan area while maintaining a geographically stable boundary. Nomadization of the Fur replenishes the Baggara, who are elsewhere becoming sedentarized. The rate, however, does *not* correlate with pressure on Fur lands — since nomadization is conditional on accumulated wealth, its rate probably decreases as Fur population pressure increases. The Fur case also demonstrates the inherent instability of some of these processes, and how limited changes can have drastic results: with the agricultural innovation of orchards over the last ten years, new investment opportunities are provided which will probably greatly reduce, or perhaps for a while even reverse, the nomadization process.

Thus, though the processes that induce change of identity are important to the understanding of most cases of ethnic interdependence, they need not be conducive to population stability. In general, however, one can argue that whenever ethnic relations are stable over long periods, and particularly where the interdependence is close, one can expect to find an approximate demographic balance. The analysis of the different factors involved in this balance is an important part of the analysis of the ethnic inter-relations in the area.

The persistence of cultural boundaries

In the preceding discussion of ethnic boundary maintenance and interchange of personnel there is one very important problem that I have left aside. We have seen various examples of how individuals and small groups, because of specific economic and political circumstances in their former position and among the assimilating group, may change their locality, their subsistence pattern, their political allegiance and form, or their household membership. This still does not fully explain why such changes lead to categorical changes of ethnic identity, leaving the dichotomized ethnic groups unaffected (other than in numbers) by the interchange of personnel. In the case of adoption and incorporation of mostly immature and in any case isolated single individuals into pre-established households, as among the Yao, such complete cultural assimilation is understandable: here every new person becomes totally immersed in a Yao pattern of relationships and expectations. In the other examples, it is less clear why this total change of identity takes place. One cannot argue that it follows from a universally imputable rule of cultural integration, so that the practice of the politics of one group or the assumption of its pattern of ecologic adaptation in subsistence and economy, entails the adoption also of its other parts and forms. Indeed, the Pathan case (Ferdinand 1967) directly falsifies this argument, in that the boundaries of the Pathan ethnic group cross-cuts ecologic and political units. Using self-identification as the critical criterion of ethnic identity, it should thus be perfectly possible for a small group of Pathans to assume the political obligations of membership in a Baluch tribe, or the agricultural and husbandry practices of Kohistanis, and yet continue to call themselves Pathans. By the same token one might expect nomadization among the Fur to lead to the emergence of a nomadic section of the Fur, similar in subsistence to the Baggara but different from them in other cultural features, and in ethnic label.

Quite clearly, this is precisely what has happened in many historical situations. In cases where it does *not* happen we see the organizing and canalizing effects of ethnic distinctions. To explore the factors responsible for the difference, let us first look at the specific explanations for the changes of identity that have been advanced in the examples discussed above.

In the case of Pathan borderlands, influence and security in the segmentary and anarchic societies of this region derive from a man's previous actions, or rather from the respect that he obtains from these acts as judged by accepted standards of evaluation. The main fora for exhibiting Pathan virtues are the tribal council, and stages for the display of hospitality. But the villager in Kohistan has a standard of living where the hospitality he can provide can hardly compete with that of the conquered serfs of neighbouring Pathans, while the client of a Baluch leader cannot speak in any tribal council. To maintain Pathan identity in these situations, to declare oneself in the running as a competitor by Pathan value standards, is to condemn oneself in advance to utter failure in performance. By assuming Kohistani or Baluch identity, however, a man may, by the same performance, score quite high on the scales that then become relevant. The incentives to a change in identity are thus inherent in the change in circumstances.

Different circumstances obviously favour different performances. Since ethnic identity is associated with a culturally specific set of value standards, it follows that there are circumstances where such an identity can be moderately successfully realized, and limits beyond which such success is precluded. I will argue that ethnic identities will not be retained beyond these limits, because allegiance to basic value standards will not be sustained where one's own comparative performance is utterly inadequate.[3] The two components in this relative measure of success are, first, the performance of others and, secondly, the alternatives open to oneself. I am not making an appeal to ecologic adaptation. Ecologic feasibility, and fitness in relation to the natural environment, matter only in so far as they set a limit in terms of sheer physical survival, which is very rarely approached by ethnic groups. What matters is how well the others, with whom one interacts and to whom one is compared, manage to perform, and what alternative identities and sets of standards are available to the individual.

Ethnic identity and tangible assets

The boundary-maintaining factors in the Fur are not immediately illuminated by this argument. Haaland (pp. 65 f.) discusses the evaluation of the nomad's life by Fur standards and finds the balance between advantages and disadvantages inconclusive. To ascertain the comparability of this case, we need to look more generally at all the factors that affect the behaviour in question. The materials derive from grossly different ethnographic contexts and so a number of factors are varied simultaneously.

The individual's relation to productive resources stands out as the significant contrast between the two regions. In the Middle East, the means of production are conventionally held as private or corporate, defined and transferable property. A man can obtain them through a specific and restricted transaction, such as purchase or lease; even in conquest the rights that are obtained are standard, delimited rights. In Darfur, on the other hand, as in much of the Sudanic belt, the prevailing conventions are different. Land for cultivation is allocated, as needed, to members of a local community. The distinction between owner and cultivator, so important in the social structure of most Middle Eastern communities, cannot be made because ownership does not involve separable, absolute, and transferable rights. Access to the means of production in a Fur village is therefore conditional only on inclusion in the village community — i.e. on Fur ethnic identity. Similarly, grazing rights are not allocated and monopolized, even as between Baggara tribes. Though groups and tribes tend to use the same routes and areas every year, and may at times try in an *ad hoc* way to keep out others from an area they wish to use, they normally intermix and have no defined and absolute prerogatives. Access to grazing is thus an automatic aspect of practising husbandry, and entails being a Baggara.

The gross mechanisms of boundary maintenance in Darfur are thus quite simple: a man has access to the critical means of production by virtue of practising a certain subsistence; this entails a whole style of life, and all these characteristics are subsumed under the ethnic labels Fur and Baggara. In the Middle East, on the other hand, men can obtain control over means of production through a transaction that does not involve their other activities; ethnic identity is then not necessarily affected and this opens the way for diversification. Thus nomad, peasant, and city dweller can belong to the same ethnic group in the Middle East; where ethnic boundaries persist they depend on more subtle and specific mechanisms, mainly connected with the unfeasibility of certain status and role combinations.

Ethnic groups and stratification

Where one ethnic group has control of the means of production utilized by another group, a relationship of inequality and stratification obtains. Thus Fur and Baggara do not make up a stratified system, since they utilize different niches and have access to them independently of each other, whereas in some parts of the Pathan area one finds stratification based on the control of land, Pathans being landowners, and other groups cultivating as serfs. In more general terms, one may say that stratified poly-ethnic systems exist where groups are characterized by differential control of assets that are valued by all groups in the system. The cultures of the component ethnic groups in such systems are thus integrated in a special way: they share certain general value orientations and scales, on the basis of which they can arrive at judgements of hierarchy.

Obversely, a system of stratification does not entail the existence of ethnic groups. Leach (1967) argues convincingly that social classes are distinguished by different sub-cultures, indeed, that this is a more basic characteristic than their hierarchical ordering. However, in many systems of stratification we are not dealing with bounded strata at all: the stratification is based simply on the notion of scales and the recognition of an ego-centered level of 'people who are just like us' versus those more select and those more vulgar. In such systems, cultural differences, whatever they are, grade into each other, and nothing like a social organization of ethnic groups emerges. Secondly, most systems of stratification allow, or indeed entail, mobility based on evaluation by the scales that define the hierarchy. Thus a moderate failure in the 'B' sector of the hierarchy makes you a 'C', etc. Ethnic groups are not open to this kind of penetration: the ascription of ethnic identity is based on other and more restrictive criteria. This is most clearly illustrated by Knutsson's analysis of the Galla in the context of Ethiopian society (pp. 86 ff.) — a social system where whole ethnic groups are stratified with respect to their positions of privilege and disability within the state. Yet the attainment of a governorship does not make an Amhara of a Galla, nor does estrangement as an outlaw entail loss of Galla identity.

From this perspective, the Indian caste system would appear to be a special case of a stratified poly-ethnic system. The boundaries of castes are defined by ethnic criteria: thus individual failures in performance lead to out-casting and not to down-casting. The process whereby the hierarchical system incorporates new ethnic groups is demonstrated in the *sanscritization of tribals:* their acceptance of the critical value scales defining their position in the hierarchy of ritual purity and pollution is the only change of values that is necessary for a people to become an Indian caste. An analysis of the different processes of boundary maintenance involved in different inter-caste relations and in different regional variants of the caste system would, I believe, illuminate many features of this system.

The preceding discussion has brought out a somewhat anomalous general feature of ethnic identity as a status: ascription[4] is not conditional on the control of any specific assets, but rests on criteria of origin and commitment; whereas *performance* in the status, the adequate acting out of the roles required to realize the identity, in many systems does require such assets. By contrast, in a bureaucratic office the incumbent is provided with those assets that are required for the performance of the role; while kinship positions, which are ascribed without reference to a person's assets, likewise are not conditional on performance — you remain a father even if you fail to feed your child.

Thus where ethnic groups are interrelated in a stratified system, this requires the presence of special processes that maintain differential control of assets. To schematize: a basic premise of ethnic group organization is that every A can act roles, 1, 2 and 3. If actors agree on this, the premise is self-fulfilling, unless acting in these roles requires assets that are distributed in a discrepant pattern. If these assets are obtained or lost in ways independent of being an A, and sought and avoided without reference to one's identity as an A, the premise will be falsified: some A's become unable to act in the expected roles. Most systems of stratification are maintained by the solution that in such cases, the person is no longer an A. In the case of ethnic identity, the solution on the contrary is the recognition that every A no longer can or will act in roles 1 and 2. The persistence of stratified poly-ethnic systems thus entails the presence of factors that generate and maintain a categorically different distribution of assets: state controls, as in some modern plural and racist systems; marked differences in evaluation that canalize the efforts of actors in different directions, as in systems with polluting occupations; or differences in culture that generate marked differences in political organization, economic organization, or individual skills.

The problem of variation

Despite such processes, however, the ethnic label subsumes a number of simultaneous characteristics which no doubt cluster statistically, but which are not absolutely interdependent and connected. Thus there will be variations between members, some showing many and some showing few characteristics. Particularly where people change their identity, this creates ambiguity since ethnic membership is at once a question of source of origin as well as of current identity. Indeed, Haaland was taken out to see 'Fur who live in nomad camps', and I have heard members of Baluch tribal sections explain that they are 'really Pathan'. What is then left of the boundary maintenance and the categorical dichotomy, when the actual distinctions are blurred in this way? Rather than despair at the failure of typological schematism, one can legitimately note that people *do* employ ethnic labels and that there are in many parts of the world most spectacular differences whereby forms of behaviour cluster so that whole actors tend to fall into such categories in terms of their objective behaviour. What is surprising is not the existence of some actors that fall between these categories, and of some regions in the world where whole persons do not tend to sort themselves out in this way, but the fact that variations tend to cluster at all. We can then be concerned not to perfect a typology, but to discover the processes that bring about such clustering.

An alternative mode of approach in anthropology has been to dichotomize the ethnographic material in terms of ideal versus actual or conceptual versus empirical, and then concentrate on the consistencies (the 'structure') of the ideal, conceptual part of the data, employing some vague notion of norms and individual deviance to account for the actual, statistical patterns. It is of course perfectly feasible to distinguish between a people's model of their social system and their aggregate pattern of pragmatic behaviour, and indeed quite necessary not to confuse the two. But the fertile problems in social anthropology are concerned with how the two are interconnected, and it does not follow that this is best elucidated by dichotomizing and confronting them as total systems. In these essays we have tried to build the analysis on a lower level of interconnection between status and behaviour. I would argue that people's categories are for acting, and are significantly affected by interaction rather than contemplation. In showing the connection between ethnic labels and the maintenance of cultural diversity, I am therefore concerned primarily to show how, under varying circumstances, certain constellations of categorization and value orientation have a self-fulfilling character, how others will tend to be falsified by experience, while others again are incapable of consummation in interaction. Ethnic boundaries can emerge and persist only in the former situation, whereas they should dissolve or be absent in the latter situations. With such a feedback from people's experiences to the categories they employ, simple ethnic dichotomies can be retained, and their stereotyped behavioural differential reinforced, despite a considerable objective variation. This is so because actors struggle to maintain conventional definitions of the situation in social encounters through selective perception, tact, and sanctions, and because of difficulties in finding other, more adequate codifications of experience. Revision only takes place where the categorization is grossly inadequate — not merely because it is untrue in any objective sense, but because it is consistently unrewarding to act upon, within the domain where the actor makes it relevant. So the dichotomy of Fur villagers and Baggara nomads is maintained despite the patent presence of a nomadic camp of Fur in the neighbourhood: the fact that those nomads speak Fur and have kinship connections with villagers somewhere does not change the social situation in which the villager interacts with them — it simply makes the standard transactions of buying milk, allocating camp sites, or obtaining manure, which one would have with other Baggara, flow a bit more smoothly. But a dichotomy between Pathan landowners and non-Pathan labourers can no longer be maintained where non-Pathans obtain land and embarrass Pathans by refusing to respond with the respect which their imputed position as menials would have sanctioned.

Minorities, pariahs, and organizational characteristics of the periphery
In some social systems, ethnic groups co-reside though no major aspect of structure is based on ethnic inter-relations. These are generally referred to as societies with minorities, and the analysis of the minority situation involves a special variant of inter-ethnic relations. I think in most cases, such situations have come about as a result of external historical events; the cultural differentiae have not sprung from the local organizational context — rather, a pre-established cultural contrast is brought into conjunction with a pre-established social system, and is made relevant to life there in a diversity of ways.

An extreme form of minority position, illustrating some but not all features of minorities, is that of pariah groups. These are groups actively rejected by the host population because of behaviour or characteristics positively condemned, though often useful in some specific, practical way. European pariah groups of recent centuries (executioners, dealers in horseflesh and -leather, collectors of nightsoil, gypsies, etc.) exemplify most features: as breakers of basic taboos they were rejected by the larger society. Their identity imposed a definition on social situations which gave very little scope for interaction with persons in the majority population, and simultaneously as an imperative status represented an inescapable disability that prevented them from assuming the normal statuses involved in other definitions of the situation of interaction. Despite these formidable barriers, such groups do not seem to have developed the internal complexity that would lead us to regard them as full-fledged ethnic groups; only the culturally foreign gypsies[5] clearly constitute such a group.

The boundaries of pariah groups are most strongly maintained by the excluding host population, and they are often forced to make use of easily noticeable diacritica to advertise their identity (though since this identity is often the basis for a highly insecure livelihood, such over-communication may sometimes also serve the pariah individual's competitive interests). Where pariahs attempt to pass into the larger society, the culture of the host population is generally well known; thus the problem is reduced to a question of escaping the stigmata of disability by dissociating with the pariah community and faking another origin.

Many minority situations have a trace of this active rejection by the host population. But the general feature of all minority situations lies in the organization of activities and interaction: In the total social system, all sectors of activity are organized by statuses open to members of the majority group, while the status system of the minority has only relevance to relations within the minority and only to some sectors of activity, and does not provide a basis for action in other sectors, equally valued in the minority culture. There is thus a disparity between values and organizational facilities: prized goals are outside the field organized by the minority's culture and categories. Though such systems contain several ethnic groups, interaction between members of the different groups of this kind does not spring from the complementarity of ethnic identities; it takes place entirely within the framework of the dominant, majority group's statuses and institutions, where identity as a minority member gives no basis for action.

though it may in varying degrees represent a disability in assuming the operative statuses. Eidheim's paper gives a very clear analysis of this situation, as it obtains among Coast Lapps.

But in a different way, one may say that in such a poly-ethnic system, the contrastive cultural characteristics of the component groups are located in the non-articulating sectors of life. For the minority, these sectors constitute a 'backstage' where the characteristics that are stigmatic in terms of the dominant majority culture can covertly be made the objects of transaction.

The present-day minority situation of Lapps has been brought about by recent external circumstances. Formerly, the important context of interaction was the local situation, where two ethnic groups with sufficient knowledge of each other's culture maintained a relatively limited, partly symbiotic relationship based in their respective identities. With the fuller integration of Norwegian society, bringing the northern periphery into the nation-wide system, the rate of cultural change increased drastically. The population of Northern Norway became increasingly dependent on the institutional system of the larger society, and social life among Norwegians in Northern Norway was increasingly organized to pursue activities and obtain benefits within the wider system. This system has not, until very recently, taken ethnic identity into account in its structure, and until a decade ago there was practically no place in it where one could participate *as a Lapp*. Lapps as Norwegian citizens, on the other hand, are perfectly free to participate, though under the dual disability of peripheral location and inadequate command of Norwegian language and culture. This situation has elsewhere, in the inland regions of Finnmark, given scope for Lappish innovators with a political program based on the ideal of ethnic pluralism (cf. Eidheim 1967), but they have gained no following in the Coast Lapp area here discussed by Eidheim. For these Lapps, rather, the relevance of Lappish statuses and conventions decreases in sector after sector (cf. Eidheim 1966), while the relative inadequacy of performance in the widest system brings about frustrations and a crisis of identity.

Culture contact and change

This is a very widespread process under present conditions as dependence on the products and institutions of industrial societies spreads in all parts of the world. The important thing to recognize is that a drastic reduction of cultural differences between ethnic groups does not correlate in any simple way with a reduction in the organizational relevance of ethnic identities, or a breakdown in boundary-maintaining processes. This is demonstrated in much of the case material. We can best analyse the interconnection by looking at the agents of change: what strategies are open and attractive to them, and what are the organizational implications of different choices on their part? The agents in this case are the persons normally referred to somewhat ethno-centrically as the new elites: the persons in the less industrialized groups with greater contact and more dependence on the goods and organizations of industrialized societies. In their pursuit of participation in wider social systems to obtain new forms of value they can choose between the following basic strategies: (i) they may attempt to pass and become incorporated in the pre-established industrial society and cultural group; (ii) they may accept a 'minority' status, accommodate to and seek to reduce their minority disabilities by encapsulating all cultural differentiae in sectors of non-articulation, while participating in the larger system of the industrialized group in the other sectors of activity; (iii) they may choose to emphasize ethnic identity, using it to develop new positions and patterns to organize activities in those sectors formerly not found in their society, or inadequately developed for the new purposes. If the cultural innovators are successful in the first strategy, their ethnic group will be denuded of its source of internal diversification and will probably remain as a culturally conservative, low-articulating ethnic group with low rank in the larger social sytem. A general acceptance of the second strategy will prevent the emergence of a clearly dichotomizing poly-ethnic organization, and — in view of the diversity of industrial society and consequent variation and multiplicity of fields of articulation — probably lead to an eventual assimilation of the minority. The third strategy generates many of the interesting movements that can be observed today, from nativism to new states.

I am unable to review the variables that affect which basic strategy will be adopted, which concrete form it may take, and what its degree of success and cumulative implications may be. Such factors range from the number of ethnic groups in the system to features of the ecologic regime and details of the constituent cultures, and are illustrated in most of the concrete analyses of the following essays. It may be of interest to note some of the forms in which ethnic identity is made organizationally relevant to new sectors in the current situation.

Firstly, the innovators may choose to emphasize one level of identity among the several provided by the traditional social organization. Tribe, caste, language group, region or state all have features that make them a potentially adequate primary ethnic identity for group reference, and the outcome will depend on the readiness with which others can be led to embrace these identities, and the cold tactical facts. Thus, though tribalism may rally the broadest support in many African areas, the resultant groups seem unable to stand up against the sanctioning apparatus even of a relatively rudimentary state organization.

Secondly, the mode of organization of the ethnic group varies, as does the inter-ethnic articulation that is sought. The fact that contemporary forms are prominently political does not make them any less ethnic in character. Such political movements constitute new ways of making cultural differences organizationally relevant (Kleivan 1967), and new ways of articulating the dichotomized ethnic groups. The proliferation of ethnically based pressure groups, political parties, and visions of independent statehood, as well as the multitude of sub-political advancement associations (Sommerfelt 1967) show the importance of these new forms. In other areas, cult-movements or mission-introduced sects are used to dichotomize and articulate groups in new ways. It is striking that these new patterns are so rarely concerned with the economic sector of activities, which is so major a factor in the culture contact situation, apart from the forms of state socialism adopted by some of the new nations. By contrast, the traditional complex poly-ethnic systems have been prominently based on articulation in this sector, through occupational differentiation and articulation at the market place in many regions of Asia and Middle America, or most elaborately, through agrarian production in South Asia. Today, contending ethnic groups not infrequently become differentiated with respect to educational level and attempt to control or monopolize educational facilities for this purpose (Sommerfelt 1967), but this is not so much with a view to occupational differentiation as because of the obvious connection between bureaucratic competence and opportunities for political advancement. One may speculate that an articulation entailing complex differentiation of skills, and sanctioned by the constant dependence on livelihood, will have far greater strength and stability than one based on revocable political affiliation and sanctioned by the exercise of force and political fiat, and that these new forms of poly-ethnic systems are probably inherently more turbulent and unstable than the older forms.

When political groups articulate their opposition in terms of ethnic criteria, the direction of cultural change is also affected. A political confrontation can only be implemented by making the groups similar and thereby comparable, and this will have effect on every new sector of activity which is made politically relevant. Opposed parties thus tend to become structurally similar, and differentiated only by a few clear diacritica. Where ethnic groups are organized in political confrontation in this way, the process of opposition will therefore lead to a reduction of the cultural differences between them.

For this reason, much of the activity of political innovators is concerned with the codification of idioms: the selection of signals for identity and the assertion of value for these cultural diacritica, and the suppression or denial of relevance for other differentiae. The issue as to which new cultural forms are compatible with the native ethnic identity is often hotly contended, but is generally settled in favour of syncretism for the reasons noted above. But a great amount of attention may be paid to the revival of select traditional culture traits, and to the establishment of historical traditions to justify and glorify the idioms and the identity.

The interconnection between the diacritica that are chosen for emphasis, the boundaries that are defined, and the differentiating values that are espoused, constitute a fascinating field for study.[6] Clearly, a number of factors are relevant. Idioms vary in their appropriateness for different kinds of units. They are unequally adequate for the innovator's purposes, both as means to mobilize support and as supports in the strategy of confrontation with other groups. Their stratificational implications both within and between groups are important: they entail different sources and distributions of influence within the group, and different claims to recognition from other groups through suppression or glorification of different forms of social stigmata. Clearly, there is no simple connection between the ideological basis of a movement and the idioms chosen; yet both have implications for subsequent boundary maintenance, and the course of further change.

Variations in the setting for ethnic relations

These modern variants for poly-ethnic organization emerge in a world of bureaucratic administration, developed communications, and progressive urbanization. Clearly, under radically different circumstances, the critical factors in the definition and maintenance of ethnic boundaries would be different. In basing ourselves on limited and contemporary data, we are faced with difficulties in generalizing about ethnic processes, since major variables may be ignored because they are not exhibited in the cases at our disposal. There can be little doubt that social anthropologists have tended to regard the rather special situation of colonial peace and external administration, which has formed the backdrop of most of the influential monographs, as if this were representative of conditions at most times and places. This may have biased the interpretation both of pre-colonial systems and of contemporary, emergent forms. The attempt in these essays to cover regionally very diverse cases is not alone an adequate defence against such bias, and the issue needs to be faced directly.

Colonial regimes are quite extreme in the extent to which the administration and its rules are divorced from locally based social life. Under such a regime, individuals hold certain rights to protection uniformly through large population aggregates and regions, far beyond the reach of their own social relationships and institutions. This allows physical proximity and opportunities for contact between persons of different ethnic groups regardless of the absence of shared understandings between them, and thus clearly removes one of the constraints that normally operate on inter-ethnic relations. In such situations, interaction can develop and proliferate — indeed, only those forms of interaction that are directly inhibited by other factors will be absent and remain as sectors of non-articulation. Thus ethnic boundaries in such situations represent a positive organization of social relations around differentiated and complementary values, and cultural differences will tend to be reduced with time and approach the required minimum.

In most political regimes, however, where there is less security and people live under a greater threat of arbitrariness and violence outside their primary community, the insecurity itself acts as a constraint on inter-ethnic contacts. In this situation, many forms of interaction between members of different ethnic groups may fail to develop, even though a potential complementarity of interests obtains. Forms of interaction may be blocked because of a lack of trust or a lack of opportunities to consummate transactions. What is more, there are also internal sanctions in such communities which tend to enhance overt conformity within and cultural differences between communities. If a person is dependent for his security on the voluntary and spontaneous support of his own community, self-identification as a member of this community needs to be explicitly expressed and confirmed; and any behaviour which is deviant from the standard may be interpreted as a weakening of the identity, and thereby of the bases of security. In such situations, fortuitous historical differences in culture between different communities will tend to perpetuate themselves without any positive organizational basis; many of the observable cultural differentiae may thus be of very limited relevance to the ethnic organization.

The processes whereby ethnic units maintain themselves are thus clearly affected, but not fundamentally changed, by the variable of regional security. This can also be shown by an inspection of the cases analysed in these essays, which represent a fair range from the colonial to the poly-centric, up to relatively anarchic situations. It is important, however, to recognize that this background variable may change very rapidly with time, and in the projection of long-range processes this is a serious difficulty. Thus in the Fur case, we observe a situation of externally maintained peace and very small-scale local political activity, and can form a picture of inter-ethnic processes and even rates in this setting. But we know that over the last few generations, the situation has varied from one of Baggara-Fur confrontation under an expansive Fur sultanate to a nearly total anarchy in Turkish and Mahdi times; and it is very difficult to estimate the effects of these variations on the processes of nomadization and assimilation, and arrive at any long-range projection of rates and trends.

Ethnic groups and cultural evolution

The perspective and analysis presented here have relevance to the theme of cultural evolution. No doubt human history is a story of the development of emergent forms, both of cultures and societies. The issue in anthropology has been how this history can best be depicted, and what kinds of analyses are adequate to discover general principles in the courses of change. Evolutionary analysis in the rigorous sense of the biological fields has based its method on the construction of phyletic lines. This method presumes the existence of units where the boundaries and the boundary-maintaining processes can be described, and thus where the continuity can be specified. Concretely, phyletic lines are meaningful because specific boundaries prevent the interchange of genetic material; and so one can insist that the reproductive *isolate* is the unit, and that it has maintained an identity undisturbed by the changes in the morphological characteristics of the species.

I have argued that boundaries are also maintained between ethnic units, and that consequently it is possible to specify the nature of continuity and persistence of such units. These essays try to show that ethnic boundaries are maintained in each case by a limited set of cultural features. The persistence of the unit then depends on the persistence of these cultural differentiae, while continuity can also be specified through the changes of the unit brought about by changes in the boundary-defining cultural differentiae.

However, most of the cultural matter that at any time is associated with a human population is *not* constrained by this boundary; it can vary, be learnt, and change without any critical relation to the boundary maintenance of the ethnic group. So when one traces the history of a ethnic group through time, one is *not* simultaneously, in the same sense, tracing the history of 'a culture': the elements of the present culture of that ethnic group have not sprung from the partic- ular set that constituted the group's culture at a previous time, whereas the group has a continual organizational existence with boundaries (criteria of membership) that despite modifications have marked off a continuing unit.

Without being able to specify the boundaries of cultures, it is not possible to construct phyletic lines in the more rigorous evolutionary sense. But from the analysis that has been argued here, it should be possible to do so for ethnic groups, and thus in a sense for those aspects of culture which have this organizational anchoring.

[1] The emphatic ideological denial of the primacy of ethnic identity (and rank) which characterises the universal religions that have arisen in the Middle East is understandable in this perspective, since practically any movement for social or ethical reform in the poly-ethnic societies of that region would clash with conven- tions and standards of ethnic character.

[2] The difference between ethnic groups and social strata, which seems problematical at this stage of the argument, will be taken up below.

[3] I am here concerned only with individual failure to maintain identity, where most members do so successfully, and not with the broader questions of cultural vitality and anomie.

[4] As opposed to presumptive classification in passing social encounters — I am thinking of the person in his normal social context where others have a considerable amount of previous information about him, not of the possibilities afforded occasion- ally for mispresenting one's identity towards strangers.

[5] The condemned behaviour which gives pariah position to the gypsies is com- pound, but rests prominently on their wandering life, originally in contrast to the serf bondage of Europe, later in their flagrant violation of puritan ethics of respon- sibility, toil and morality.

[6] To my knowledge, Mitchell's essay on the Kalela dance (Mitchell 1956) is the first and still the most penetrating study on this topic.

When Ethnic Identity is a Social Stigma

by Harald Eidheim

The problem of delimiting ethnic groups as contrasting cultural units, and of defining ethnic borders, has occupied many anthropologists, in particular many of the cultural anthropological school. The distribution of cultural and other 'objective' traits has usually been the empirical evidence on which their approaches have been built. Analyses of such data may provide us with a statistical and distributive picture (if it is possible to agree on a definition of *a trait*) and may show how the concentration of traits correlates with named groups. However, if ethnic groups should not happen to coincide with contrasting economic systems or with firm and enduring political groups, there will always be the problem of 'transitional zones', i.e. where such criteria give ill-defined ethnic borders. Yet in many such areas, people themselves apparently have no difficulties in ascribing ethnic membership, i.e. we might find a high degree of 'homogeneity' (rather insignificant distribution of objective traits) but still indications of ethnic diversity, expressed in native theory and also articulated in the routine of interpersonal behaviour (cf. Nadel 1947, Garvin 1958, Moerman 1965.

This poses the general problem of how ethnic diversity is socially articulated and maintained.

To analyse the social organization of ethnic borders we need a relational frame of reference, in which we can single out those objective phenomena that we somewhat dubiously called 'traits', by concepts logically consistent with a relational language. The basic axiom for such analyses is that ethnic groups are social categories which provide a basis for status ascription, and consequently that inter-ethnic relations are organized with reference to such statuses. My material shows a situation where an ethnic status (or identity) is, in a sense, illegitimate, and therefore not acted out in institutional inter-ethnic behaviour. Nevertheless, this very illegitimacy has definite implications in the process of role-taking in elementary interaction and thus adds form to inter-ethnic relations.

My case refers to an area of mixed Norwegian — Coast Lappish population inhabiting the fjords and inlets of West-Finnmark, Northern Norway.[1] Throughout West-Finnmark there is a conspicuous lack of 'contrasting cultural traits' between Lapps and Norwegians, but these ethnic labels are attached to communities as well as to families and individual persons, and are in daily use. The consistent, though not public use of such labels indicates that an ethnic identity is a topic of importance in the relationships between persons carrying contrasting as well as similar identities. The language of symbols which bear on an identity cleavage is rich and finely shaded. I have been able to understand and analyze only the gross forms of these symbols and their differentiating significance. It is fairly evident, however, that very few of them may be classified as contrasting traits with reference to ethnic provenance, the mother tongue dichotomy (Lapp-Norwegian) being perhaps the only obvious contrast. The language of symbols thus must be understood in a local social context; we are faced with the difficult task of understanding the local mode of valuation and interpretation of general behaviour expressed in such terms as, for instance, self-sufficiency, covertness, politeness, or cleanliness.

Under the disability of a stigmatized ethnic identity, members of the Coast Lappish population in question seek to qualify themselves as full participants in the Norwegian society. In order to obtain this membership they have to develop techniques to avoid or tolerate sanctions from the local Norwegian population. In the following I hope to be able to show that the behavioural forms which under such constraints are displayed on the stages of everyday life, are organized in distinct spheres of interaction which articulate and maintain an identity dichotomy. Spheres of interaction as well as identities emerge through everyday interaction because impression management about identities is of constant concern to the actors.

Let me now turn more concretely to the ethnic situation in Finnmark, the northernmost county in Norway.

In the townships (Norw. *kommuner*) of the inland region, which are the strongholds of Lappish culture in Norway, the Lappish speaking population constitutes an 80–90 per cent majority. The Norwegian part of the population is engaged in various administrative and social services and in commerce. Some of these Norwegians are bilingual, as is the Lappish population in general. Of a population of more than 8,000, fifteen per cent are Reindeer Lapps. These live in their permanent houses while their herds are on their winter pastures in the vicinity, but most of them leave the region in summer when they stay with their herds on headlands and islands along the Arctic coast. The reindeer population in the region is slightly above 100,000 head (Aarseth 1967). The great bulk of the Lappish population pursue dairy farming and have inland fishing and cloudberry picking as subsidiary occupations. Quite a few are also engaged in social and administrative services and in transportation.

As one moves from the interior towards the townships of the fjord and coast area, the ethnic proportions of the population are reversed. The proportion of Lappish speakers in some townships is inconsiderable, while in others it might amount to 20–25 per cent. (The only exception is one fjordal township in East Finnmark with a 50/50-constellation.) Lapps as well as Norwegians combine farming and fishing with no difference in ecologic adaptation along ethnic lines. Spatially, however, there is a tendency to ethnic clustering. The towns and fishing villages on the coast are entirely dominated by Norwegians (cf. Vorren (ed.) 1963, Kirke- og undervisningsdepartementet 1959). In the fjord area and especially in the western part which concerns us here, visible signs of Lappishness, which prevail e.g. in the inland region, are either absent in the indigenous population, (as are reindeer herding and nomad life, Lappish costume and the public use of Lappish language) or they are rather unreliable criteria for classification of individual persons (as is physical type).[2] People make a living from fishing and small farming in the same way as in peripheral settlements all along the North Norwegian coast. Clothing, food habits, housing, the major forms of social institutions, ideals and values are also so evenly distributed that there are seemingly only trivial differences from one locality to another. In short, an outsider, paying a casual and short visit in the area, will most likely notice no signs of ethnic diversity, not to speak of an ethnic border.

Such were also my own first impressions as a field worker. I knew, of course, that I was on the edges of the Lappish area, but my eyes and ears told me that I was inside a Norwegian fjord community. It was not until I was able to observe and learn from the daily events of my own socialization into the community that I became sensitized to the relational aspect of the local ethnic dichotomy. I will therefore take the liberty of reviewing some of the initial, and, I think, important phases of this process, leaving aside the obvious traumatic aspects caused by my own blunders.

At first I was merely looked upon as some kind of travelling Norwegian, maybe a somewhat unusual one, because a visit from a complete stranger who has no definite and conventional task is an extremely rare occasion. In any case, I was a person towards whom people in the community considered it appropriate to show off their Norwegianness. They made efforts to underline this quality of theirs by communicating their competence in modern fishing and agriculture, and by telling about local public events which they thought meritorious with reference to this quality. Many people liked to stress that they were well travelled and pretended to have a good knowledge of other parts of Norway, and they did not forget to mention that people from this fjord were settled as far away as Oslo, Germany, Alaska, and Australia. In addition, they liked to dwell on their good standard of housing, and the quality of their stables compared to what they had seen during their evacuation period 1944/45 farther south. (All the buildings in this area were burnt down by the Germans in 1944 and the population evacuated, but the communities were rebuilt and resettled through a governmental aid program after the war.) Housewives constantly took pride in showing their well-furnished kitchens. They also had what to me seemed to be a craze for cleanliness, and entertained me for hours about their precautions and good habits in their daily housekeeping. (In local Norwegian native theory, uncleanliness is one of the vices of the Lapps.)

All this was communicated in the local Norwegian dialect which all spoke quite well, but which very few, if any, had a perfect command of, since the structure of Lappish to some extent, is likely to invade their speech and produce a slightly broken Norwegian. This is even true in those homes in the community which have abandoned the Lappish language (see below).

I have mentioned a few themes which local people were eager to pursue in our conversations. As mere themes they are conventional in normal Norwegian discourse, and might be thought sociologically unimportant. But it was the recurrent management of these themes, combined with the fact that themes which pointed to ethnic differentiation in the population were obviously avoided, which eventually led me to look upon them as a vital part of a process of presentation of identity (cf. Goffman 1959). This became more evident to me as my socialization proceeded into the next stage.

Gradually I accentuated my interests in the Lappish population and cautiously presented myself more concretely by telling about my studies and reproducing what is recorded in books about the area, and I apparently added depth and concreteness to their image of me as a most unusual Norwegian. Needless to say, however, my interests and questions annoyed most people in the community. Some young people avoided me for weeks when rumours about my interests spread through kitchen conversations; they took me for some sort of unpleasant detective. Others, notably some of the middle-aged, took me into their confidence. I was concerned with Lapps in a way which they could perceive as being far from negative, and I appeared to be a useful source of information about the wider society. (Other anthropologists have, of course, experienced similar field situations.) Regarding me little by little as an acceptable stranger, uncommitted on controversies about ethnicity, people became more relaxed in their relations with me. They became more careless with the 'secret' that they habitually used Lappish in their daily life, and when they also discovered that I could join in a simple conversation in Lappish, we had established such relations that I was able to broach the question of ethnicity more openly and directly than before. The themes of discussion which were current in my initial socialization faded more and more into the background. However, except within separate households and small groups of three–four persons, I was never able to engage people in discussion about these matters. In public encounters, such as parties which 10–15 people attended, in the small crowds of customers gathered at the merchant's shop or in the crowd waiting on the quay for the local steamer, I had little success.

In short, this first groping phase of my field work, which also brought me to neighbouring communities, including the administrative centre of the township, led me eventually to some basic social facts which were at odds with the façade that people presented as long as they regarded me as an ordinary Norwegian.

These facts were:

1. People in the area have a good personal knowledge of each other, and can classify each other very precisely as either Lapp or Norwegian (or *finn* versus *dáža* which are the labels in Norwegian and Lappish respectively).

This is true only within local districts: I define *the district*, with reference to interaction and communication, as the area within which people have mutual personal knowledge of place of residence, heritage, doings and personal inclinations. Thus, we have to visualize the district from the point of view of a central fixed point, which in this case is *the fjord community* where I concentrated my field-work. Obviously, the district so defined has no definite borders; it represents a concentration in a field of personal information; but for the present purpose we may say that within a diffuse range of 30–50 kilometers it encompasses scattered, small communities of from one or two households up to a hundred or more which people think of as inhabited by Lapps and Norwegians in various proportions. The fjord community in which I worked was one of the most Lappish with only six persons out of ca. 150 classified as Norwegians, and the administrative centre of the township being the most Norwegian with about 20 out of 300 classified as Lapps.

2. In this fjord community, Lappish was the domestic language in about 40 of the 50 odd households. In each of the ten which used Norwegian, at least one person knew Lappish and used it in other social contexts. Outside the households Lappish was a medium of communication within the wider district, but language behaviour is such that Lappish must be regarded as a secret language or code, regularly used only in situations where trusted Lappish identities are involved.

Having grasped these facts, which clearly indicated that the question of Lappish identity was a topic of general concern, and having realized that the dimension of social space must be a promising frame of observations, I could engage in more selective data collecting.

Not surprisingly, my best friends among the Lapps in the fjord at this point started admitting me to their personal dilemmas of identity. This would often take the form of confessions: They were after all a kind of Lapp. Their parents and grandparents lived in turf huts, some of them as late as the 1930s. Some people even wore Lappish costumes at that time, and Lappish foot-wear was in common use until World War II. They were bothered by not being fully proficient in Norwegian and by the spite and ridicule to which they were often exposed for this and other reasons in interactions with self-confident and arrogant Norwegians. They even had the suspecion that their low standard of living and the lack of industrial enterprises in the fjord might derive from their being of an inferior race.[3] 'The Lapps must be stupid', they said. Certainly they believed the average Norwegian to be of that opinion. In all details their miserable self-image was a reflection of the Lappish stigma as local Norwegians define it.

This dilemma appeared to be most developed in persons from 16–17 up to 50, the age classes where aspirations are strongest; a psychiatrist would probably say that this part of the population was subject to an identity-neurosis. In my article on guest relationships (Eidheim 1966) I have described how people in this fjord behave towards Nomad Lapps. Displaying their preference for contract relations, their new and comfortable houses, their cleanliness and their command of Norwegian, the fjord dwellers very ostentatiously act out a 'Norwegian' identity. However, as is understood, the relationships with people whom they themselves classify as *dážat* (Norwegians) show quite another aspect of their situation.

In very general terms one may say that the basis for their dilemma is that in order to achieve the material and social goods they appreciate, and to share the opportunities available in the society, people have to get rid of, or cover up, those social characteristics which Norwegians take as signs of Lappishness.

This must be understood on the background of certain traits of local ecology and society.[4] Local resources, the amount of arable soil and the local fishing grounds give little or no opportunities for increased or diversified production. Capital management beyond the level of single households is non-existent (the only exception is the local private shopkeeper), nor have any other forms of associations or corporations, which could have promoted social differentiation in the neighbourhood society, gained foothold.[5] Only very few households can, or are willing to, live exclusively within the confines of neighbourhood and kin relations or exclusively from local fishing and the yields of their small farms (a cow or two and four-six sheep). A wide range of attainments therefore can only be secured through careers or at least temporary wage work, outside the fjord community, in situations where Norwegians are their social partners and where these also possess or assume the positions of formal and informal authority.

Apart from *guest*-relations with members of a nomadic unit (Eidheim 1966), these fjord dwellers have no relations with Lapps in the inland regions. They never go there, they are indifferent to the debate about the Lappish minority situation in mass media and they are outside the influence of the Lappish movement which works for consolidation and promotion of an ethnic *esprit de corps*. Their orientation and their social aspirations are confined to a social landscape where the actors are either people of Norwegian identity or people in the same opportunity situation as themselves.

The preceding description indicates that interaction is organized here in three distinct spheres, namely (1) a public sphere, (2) a Lappish closed sphere, and (3) a Norwegian closed sphere. Each of these is associated with characteristic codes, themes, and valuations, and further distinguished by the ethnic composition of the acting personnel. The spheres in their generalized forms emerge as an organizational result of ethnic heritage in this particular dual context. Situationally, however, behaviour belonging in one or another of these spheres is dependent on definable circumstances or opportunity situations.

There is first the public sphere of interaction. Inside the fjord community, the most common encounters belonging in this sphere are occasions where one or more of the local Norwegians participate. Infrequently, these are big celebrations like weddings, funerals, and baptisms; more commonly they are encounters in the routine of daily life in the community. All formally organized activity at the local public school also belongs in this sphere. Not surprisingly, therefore, a wide sector of daily encounters outside the school where children and teenagers are involved also has these public overtones: the Norwegian code is used and themes and valuations are those of the public sphere.[6]

People in the fjord community think it is 'necessary' and therefore 'right' to speak Norwegian to children. 'They shall not have the same handicap as we have had,' they say. Interaction among the small crowd of customers at the merchant's shop also belongs to the public sphere. Even when no Norwegians are present (the merchant is a local Lapp) people regard it as appropriate to define the situation as public. The merchant himself is the apparent initiator and he bluntly answers in Norwegian if it happens that someone asks a question in Lappish.

As already suggested the verbal code in this sphere of interaction is local Norwegian. The themes around which the interactions are concentrated are domestic work and the conventional problems of daily life inside the fjord community as well as outside, and the valuations are those which fit in with North Norwegian coast culture.

When people are temporarily outside the fjord they likewise define interactions with Norwegians as events in the public sphere. Locals, both Norwegians and Lapps, present themselves behaviouristically in the idioms of this sphere, and, as I have described above, they tried to constrain me by these conventions as long as they regarded me as a stranger.

Of course, the public sphere must also be defined with reference to the social properties or behaviour which are excluded from it. This behaviour is first and foremost the use of Lappish language, secondly themes, stories, and other possible pointers to the ethnic dichotomy and other actions which are regarded as the presentation of a Lappish identity. For a Norwegian explicitly to present himself as a Norwegian and to draw attention to the ethnic dichotomy is less uncommon and somewhat more legitimate than the corresponding behaviour by a Lapp, since it is implicit in the process of role-taking in public situations and congruent with a Norwegianizing intent (cf. fn. 6). Let me turn to some examples for purposes of illustration.

Per, a Lapp from the fjord community, is a member of the township's school board, which has its regular meetings in the administrative centre of the township. But he never argues in these meetings for a Lappish oriented public school in his community, nor does he suggest to fellow passengers on board the local steamer that the state has forgotten the Coast Lapps in its program for economic development of the outlying districts.

Why then, is Per recognized as a Lapp? To answer this question we must go to the syndrome of signs which the Norwegians look for. This syndrome or image is much of the same order as the term *stigma* used by Goffman (cf. Goffman 1963). There are a very great number of such signs and they are unevenly distributed among individuals. In the case of Per we might list some of the most relevant ones: (1) He comes from a certain community, which Norwegians call by a name which is a slight twist of its proper name, and which gives it an oblique derogatory edge. We might say that by this nickname persons are associated with a spatial criterion of Lappishness. (2) He has what is considered to be Lappish physiognomy. (3) He speaks a slightly broken Norwegian. (4) He seldom plays an active role in the discussions at the school board meetings. (5) He misses the meetings more often than the average member and does not instruct a deputy to go in his place. (6) 'He sticks to his own.' This is demonstrated even at the administrative centre where he frequently visits a household which is regarded as Lappish.[7]

Per and a couple of other persons from the area experience the school board meetings as a confrontation with people of Norwegian identity. A common Norwegian fisherman and the inspector of the school, though dissimilar in many respects, are in another and more vital sense the same sort of person. Per thinks that they know the nuances of suitable behaviour and effective action better than he himself, and objectively they have a fuller command of the code. They *have* the right identity, which makes them authorized initiators in the situation, while he is only some kind of satellite.

What has been said so far about the public sphere of interaction enables us to sum up some of its characteristics. Most conspicuous among these is the fact that interaction in this sphere takes place within the statuses and institutions of the dominant Norwegian population. However, it is an overruling axiom that the local population is made up of two ethnic categories, Lapps and Norwegians. Since public presentation of a Lappish identity is not an alternative, it follows that in this sphere there is no institutionalized interaction in which a status 'Lapp' has accepted roles, i.e. Lapp and Norwegian are not complementary statuses. What perpetuates the axiom of an identity cleavage, then, is the fact that people are able to identify each other as belonging to separate categories on the basis of their performance of any role in the public sphere. This reinforces the syndrome of signs attached to ethnic categories as well as the notion that separate identities are mirrored in the social landscape. Against this background we can understand that to be a Lapp is a primary restriction on impression management to the extent that all Coast Lapps avoid as much as possible behaviour which in the local language of symbols and signs points to their identity.

Such public encounters between Coast Lapps and Norwegians are part of the daily routine in the area, in all places where people meet and interact. It might be said that a pseudo-agreement on a shared identity is established when the mutually recognized pragmatic content of the relations in the public sphere is not severely violated. (The degree of severity must of course be subject to a situational definition.) The seemingly unproblematic flow of interaction in the public sphere, or the fact that the flow goes on, indicates that the gross qualities of public encounters reflect mutual agreement, and to strangers the two parties seem to communicate adequately.[8] However, each party turns to ethnically closed stages to interpret and discuss the idiomatic content of public encounters with reference to identity. The Lappish closed stages, which I made most effort to observe, constitute a sphere of interaction that can only be understood in relation to the public sphere. It is in the articulation between these two, i.e. in the routine of establishment of public stages versus ethnically closed stages that the organizational significance of identity emerges most clearly.

I think it might be a defensible simplification to leave out a full treatment of the Norwegians' closed stages, i.e. to take them more or less for granted, and concentrate upon the Lappish ones. As indicated above, in my review of the fieldworker's socialization I was successively admitted to this sphere of interaction, if not as a full participant, then at least as a harmless bystander.

The Lappish closed sphere coincides with kin and neighbourhood relations between Lapps but it also includes relations between non-kin and non-neighbours within the wider district who are known to be Lappish. Lappish language is the code of interaction. Failure to use Lappish in such interaction is sanctioned negatively, except in the case of the youngsters who have little or no command of the language. In view of the Lapps' participation also in the public sphere, and the preference for use of a stigmatizing code between neighbours/kinsfolk/friends, it is obvious that the daily round of encounters calls for a quick social apprehension and the command of shared and smooth techniques to define and redefine situations.

A most common occurrence in daily life inside the community was the entry of one of the local Norwegians into a pre-established closed stage. People then immediately switched from Lappish to Norwegian, and themes of conversation were adjusted. The Norwegians not only regard Lappish as an inferior language in a general sense, but also judge it highly improper and challenging if it is used in their presence. (All Norwegians are monolingual.) Now, of course, it happens frequently that local Norwegians are within earshot of the performance in such closed stages and they are thus regularly reminded of what kind of people they live among. Norwegians also let me into their closed stages in order to 'deepen' my understanding of the Lappish syndrome as it prevailed in their own minds and to contrast it to what they considered to be Norwegian character.[9]

At home in the fjord, the technique of changing code and theme is not felt to be very inconvenient; interaction in the closed sphere can always be resumed later. Other circumstances, however, require other solutions. The steamer on the fjordal route was a forum of considerable social importance. Here people exchanged news and gossip and here they met acquaintances as well as strangers; Norwegians and Lapps mingled. One might expect people in this setting to interact in any or all of three capacities: (a) as passengers, defining stages according to the conventions of the public sphere. (b) as Norwegians, defining closed stages of passengers, and (c) as Lapps, likewise defining closed stages of passengers. What can be observed empirically, however, is almost imperceptible transitions from (a) to (b) and vice versa (exchange of eloquent glances, pregnant silence or verbal twists which are a kind of meta-communication in plain speech). On the other hand there is a fairly high frequency of unmistakable transitions from (a) to (c) and vice versa, although the crowding on board a little boat offers few opportunities for spatial arrangements in order to avoid leakages. When a Lapp has played the role of passenger for a while with both Lapps and Norwegians as role partners, he is inclined to switch to the role of kinsman/friend in order to interact with a fellow-passenger, a Lappish person he perhaps has not met for six months or more. They both wish to exchange greetings and information in Lappish and they provisionally separate themselves spatially from the public stage. Thus, groups of two or three may for a few minutes carry on a low-voiced conversation in Lappish in a corridor, on a staircase landing or close together along the rail if the weather is not too bad. The next moment, if a person with Norwegian or uncertain identity approaches, the situation is smoothly redefined to a public one before the intruder is within earshot.

The dynamics of interaction on board the coastal steamer may serve as an illustration of some crucial points. The average public situation offers a near optimum for Norwegians to realize their spectrum of intentions, and the maintenance of a Norwegian identity is not a question of serious concern. The Lapp, on the other hand, may find himself in a serious dilemma. If he ignores Lapps, in the sense that he continues to act as passenger in the idioms of the public sphere, his kin/neighbour/friend relations with such persons will suffer; and if he avoids encounters in the public sphere in favour of such kin/neighbour/friend relations, he will be considered a covert Lapp, even if he should be successful in controlling the audio-space.

Some crucial negative statements can be deduced logically from this contrast, and may also be observed empirically: the totality of passengers never divide into two permanent or semi-permanent groups with reference to identity; nor will the simultaneous performance of roles belonging to the public sphere and the Lappish sphere ever be observed.

Given a situation of some duration where people of Lappish and Norwegian identity come together for some purpose, alternation or switching between situations of a public Norwegian type and a closed Lappish type will invariably take place if the audio-space can be controlled. A work situation that I witnessed a few times was when a carrier came to the fjord to load dried fish. Five or six local men were engaged in the work together with the Norwegian crew of three, whose main job was the trimming of the vessel. The spatial setting was a boat alongside the quay with a relatively big storehouse on the shoreside where the fish was kept. On the quay among themselves and in direct interaction with the crew on the quay edge, the local men used Norwegian, inside the storehouse they used Lappish; they switched every time they passed the door.

We have seen how the stigma of Lappishness is related to performance on public stages as well as to unintentional leakages from their ethnically homogeneous closed stages. There is also a third but uncommon variant: situations where one of the parties is so much offended that, in anger, he gives up all pretences, and an overt inter-ethnic quarrel results. Inevitably, the Norwegians have as a rule the last word in such quarrels and the Lapps are the losers. Let me review a couple of incidents which exemplify this. A man from the fjord, one of eight siblings, was educated as a school teacher. For some years he held a position in a community in East Finnmark, known to people in West Finnmark to be a Lappish dominated community; and when a vacancy occurred at his home fjord he applied for appointment there. This represented a challenge to the Norwegian dominated school board who appeared to be against having a Lappish teacher in a Lappish community. In their opinion the former Norwegian teacher had carried on successful work of Norwegianization in the fjord, and they were afraid that the new man might reverse this. A member of the school board is reported to have said, in a public situation: 'Let him just stay on there in East Finnmark together with the Lapps, he really fits in with conditions there . . .' He did not get the job.

The Norwegians' authority to define behavioural standards, even, for instance, in such a dignified institution as the school-board or in a public place like the coastal steamer, is never questioned publicly by the Lapps. But all Norwegians are not granted equal authority to define situations and set standards. One man, who came to the fjord through an uxorilocal marriage, exemplifies this situation. He accentuated his Norwegianness very arrogantly and busied himself with leakage-rumour about neighbouring Lapps. Most people in the fjord were provoked by him, and occasionally when he was alone among a plurality of local Lapps, his definition of the situation and role play would be destroyed by some of the participants. Thus one day he set out together with a few of the local Lapps to build a small bridge across a brook. As usual he pretended to be the only expert in the gang, but the others challenged his expertise and an argument developed. Once the breach was obvious, the Lapps switched to Lappish and continued the work according to their own design. The Norwegian, now almost out of his mind with rage, waved his arms and shouted insults and curses against the others; but their front was unbreakable. In a few hours he had had enough and left the place in great indignation, having confirmed the truth in the familiar North-Norwegian laconism: 'There is a (real) difference between people and Lapps.' *(Det er forskjell på folk og finn).* This incident exemplifies the rare situations where Lappish 'ethnic solidarity' is stressed in public.

Although rare, such incidents have definite and often long lasting effects. They are remembered, recapitulated and interpreted in ethnically homogeneous closed stages, and they reinforce the Norwegians' jealous search for any signs of Lappish uppishness, while to the Lapps each incident represents a reminder to be more cautious in their roleplay in the public sphere. A general feature of Lappish behaviour in the public sphere is therefore an effort to avoid provocation. The Lapp is often either a rather passive partner or he grants Norwegians extravagant role support by being servile and manageable. If he anticipates confrontations which may focus upon his identity he is apt to withdraw, avoid persons, or even to change place of work.[10]

The fact that the flow of interaction in the public sphere goes on does not indicate that the relations are based on mutual and real agreement about a shared identity. One may easily be misled to believe this, but we must realize that an inherent quality of the public sphere is that it gives no scope for Lapps to show behaviour which springs from their Lappish identity without great social costs. Such behaviour is reserved for closed stages, where the social dangers and defeats that people have been subject to in public encounters are redundantly reviewed and to some extent mended, or at least made temporarily less severe, through the sharing of adversities with other Lapps. Hourlong conversations will take place, as for instance when an adult man came home from 2–3 months' work outside the community, dropped down into a chair in the kitchen, and blurted out: 'It is fine to be able to speak Lappish again and not to be constantly cautious about how to express myself in Norwegian.' Or a Lapp might rail against the boss (something he could never do face to face) who gave him the worst jobs and made hints about his being a Lapp when he thought the job was not properly done. Others respond with old stories, and thus the conversation goes on and on.

We have now seen how persons indirectly identify each other in institutional behaviour in the public sphere and how Lapps also from time to time expose their identity in non-institutional encounters. We have also seen how indirect the sanctions are, i.e. it is clearly the anticipation of future role dilemmas and not direct sanctions which delimits and thereby adds form to the conventional roles played by Lapps in public situations. This contrasts with the clear public confrontation between the two ethnic categories that is seen in the inland regions of Finnmark (cf. the mobilization of clients in the entrepreneur case (Eidheim 1963) and the programmatic idealization of pluralism which is the basis of the nativistic Lappish movement (Eidheim 1968)). In this area a Lappish identity is not only relevant in inter-ethnic relations in the daily routine of public interpersonal behaviour, it is also claimed and made relevant in the more formalized sectors of social life, i.e. on boards and committees on township and higher levels of administration. Furthermore, it is expressed in mass media and in voluntary associations, and it is displayed in a growing cult of Lappish nativistic idioms like language, dress, folk songs, and cultural history.

Compared with this general picture of the inland regions, a Lappish identity in the Coast-Lappish area described here has very limited organizational potential. It is only relevant on closed stages which are established under the protective constraints of limited time and space. Lappish co-activity in the inland regions is a public affair which also allows the maximization and defence of Lappish values; in the coastal area, however, the manipulation of time and space in order to establish closed stages, and what goes on on these stages, may rather be understood as techniques to hide, but thereby also to sustain, a disability (or stigma) which people cannot escape.

I have used the term *sphere of interaction* to conceptualize 'public life' and 'Lappish secret life' respectively. One might alternately use the term *network* and define network as a field of relations in which exchangeable values flow, thus taking exchange in a wide and behavouristic sense. Networks emerge then as a consequence of the local distribution of exchange resources in the population.

Exchange resources in this sense are part of the social landscape (provenance, kinship relations, physiognomy, etc.) and they are recognizable in people's actions (command of language, role-taking etc.). The Lapps' exchange resources may also be effected by leakages from closed stages and occasional inter-ethnic quarrels. The existence of a Lappish network indicates that there are exchange resources which can only be marketed to certain persons, i.e. to persons of one's own identity, while the public network shows the field of relations where the exchange is such that ethnic identity is overlooked, through tact on the part of the Norwegians and covering on the part of the Lapps.

Both parties try to behave as if ethnicity 'does not count'; however, we have the paradoxical situation that it is ethnic status which underlies and delimits relations in the public network. In this network persons of different identities interact in conventional and narrowly defined role-dyads or role-clusters, and there are 'agreements' on exchange if pragmatic and proximate ends are fulfilled. It is for instance very unlikely that a Norwegian merchant will obstruct customer/merchant relations because he knows where a customer comes from, or because the customer makes grammatical errors when asking for a commodity. Quite another thing is the type of relations where 'whole persons' are involved. By and large such intimate relations are only consummated between persons of the same identity. Within the local area, a Lapp might establish such a relation with a Norwegian. Those who have a perfect command of Norwegian, and a Norwegian physiognomy, have the best chances of doing this, especially if they are willing to cut themselves off from intimate interaction with other Lapps. This indicates that in such relations ethnic idioms rank highly among the exchange resources. To pursue the above illustration: the merchant's daughter would not think of marrying a man from a stigmatized Lappish community, who in addition has a Lappish physiognomy and makes grammatical errors.[11]

It is implicit in such terms as 'district' and 'social landscape' that exchange resources are in part conditioned by local knowledge and valuations and to this extent only locally valid. Thus chances to pass can be improved by moving out.[12] If a person has other exchange resources and is willing to settle in a Norwegian community or a town outside his district there are certainly better possibilities to establish and consummate intimate or comprehensive relations with Norwegians. I have mentioned above that there is historical evidence to show that the synchronic situation depicted here represents a phase in a long range and directional process of assimilation (Norwegianization). This long range process of de-stigmatization of total Lappish communities is of course a more complex and intriguing problem than the *ex area* Norwegianization of individual persons. I have not myself done field work in communities which earlier — say hundred years ago — were regarded as Lappish but are now Norwegian; such communities are on record. What I can conclude about such processes is therefore only a deduction from the present analysis.

It would seem as if Lappish closed stages represent a necessary solution to a series of dilemmas as long as people's behaviour reinforces a cognitive dualistic system in the local Norwegian population. This system also constitutes a charter of identification and a mode of sanctioning. People in the Lappish fjord community, with their aspirations directed towards participation in the public network as it is defined by Norwegians, do what they can to present themselves as full-fledged participants. Many families have even made the drastic decision to prevent their children from learning Lappish. Presumably, as their performance in Norwegian language improves, there will be a concomitant decrease in the reinforcing effect of their behaviour upon the charter of identification which in turn brings about a reduction in sanctions. Likewise one would expect a decrease in the necessity to maintain a Lappish network as the principal field for intimate relations and as stages where social costs may be shared.

However, it is not only actual behaviour in *this* district and community which has repercussions on the local charter of identification. This is also affected by the great variety of public display of Lappishness in the wider Lappish population, for instance in the inland area of the county. As the notion of physical descent is linked to Lappish behaviour, one would suppose that a Lappish stigma on this particular community will prevail in some rudimentary form even generations after the complete abandonment of the Lappish language, granted that a flourishing Lappish culture is maintained in the inland.

What is said here about the long range process is tentative and has obvious limitations. But we need to consider the question of long range persistence of ethnic cleavages, something which usually is not exposed in the day-to-day processes we observe in the field situation. Based on precisely that kind of material it has been my main intention to analyze the dynamics of inter-ethnic relations in a population where institutionalized inter-ethnic relations are *not* organized with reference to the respective ethnic status directly, but which nevertheless are shaped by them. It is in some sense an analogue to a shadow play. The behavioural forms which have classificatory significance for the actors can only be understood by uncovering and systematizing local values and sanctions. The behavioural forms may be 'objective', as for instance language, or they may be implications of the general character of inter-ethnic behaviour as role-taking. The organizational potential of separate identities is clearly indicated in the stages of everyday life. We must bear in mind that it is the general character of *local* ecology and society which provide the meaningful context in which a Lappish/ Norwegian ethnic dichotomy is articulated. The organizational potential of ethnic identities is conditioned by local circumstances. Thus the local context of Reindeer Lapps/marginal Norwegian farmers, which for instance prevails in the southern Lapp districts of Norway, will generate quite other patterns of inter-ethnic relations (cf. Falkenberg 1964).

¹ The author did field work here for five months in 1960 and has earlier published an article on social relations between coast Lapps and Nomad Lapps in the district (Eidheim 1966).
² In some localities, however, like the fjord community where I lived during most of my field work, there is a certain concentration of what is currently understood to be the Lappish physical type.
³ And they also had other 'secrets' which they now unveiled to me; preferences for dishes which were regarded as Lappish, some old people preferred to eat with their fingers, and three or four of these also used Lappish fur moccasins (but only in their houses). Most people had put coins and other amulets into the foundations of their new houses and they also used certain spells when slaughtering, the first time they set their nets after New Year, etc.
⁴ See also Eidheim (1966).
⁵ Attempts to establish and run local branches of various national associations have been made at intervals since the beginning of this century, usually promoted by teachers or other *dážat*. However, all attempts have been short-lived. This is in contrast to the material presented by Robert Paine from another Lappish Coast fjord (cf. Paine 1965).
⁶ The school aims exclusively at communicating those values which are current in an idealized Norwegian society, and for generations it has had the implicit goal (at times also explicit) to Norwegianize the Lappish communities (Dahl 1957). Norwegian teachers and the few Norwegians who have married into the community have always assumed the role of agents in the process of Norwegianization, i. e. they have defined the behaviour standards in the public sphere.
⁷ Only very few adult Lappish persons in the district do not show traces of one or more of the stigmata listed under 1, 2, 3 and 6; as a rule they exhibit all these. In addition local Norwegians enrich the syndrome e. g. by referring to concrete role-behaviour which in their opinion demonstrates that Lapps are secretive, superstitious, stupid, etc.
⁸ In fact, if we add a time perspective we will easily see how the public sphere progressively has taken on new dimensions in the last generations. This, of course, is an indication of the directional and long range process we call assimilation.
⁹ An example: One of them said, speaking about housing: 'I made up my mind not

to accept these drawings of standard houses. It did cost me a lot of extra money, but I wanted to show them what a real house looks like and how it is to be furnished.' He was the only one in the community who had built a house with a concrete basement under the whole house. The house was built on an elevated site, and he had painted the lower part of it in a bold pink colour. 'Of course,' he said, 'people here have good houses now (you would not believe how they lived before the War) but remember that the administration forced these standard houses on them: if you come back here in a few years time you may learn something about the way they have kept them!'

[10] However, Norwegians behave with considerable 'tact' in public relations. They point out in private to me or to each other that 'yes, he is a Lap, but he is all right.' A teacher said: 'I know that many of my pupils are Lapps, of course, I have the tact not to take notice of the fact.'

[11] It is symptomatic that five out of six persons with a Norwegian identity who have married into the fjord, come from communities outside the district.

[12] Such emigration, especially by young unmarried people, takes place, but not to the extent that the population is drained off from the community.

Economic Determinants
in Ethnic Processes

by Gunnar Haaland

This essay describes and analyses processes of boundary maintenance between two of the major ethnic groups in Western Sudan: the Fur and the Baggara. I shall discuss the nature of ethnic identities and the determinants in change of identity. In the discussion I shall draw on data collected during one year's field work in the Lower Wadi Zone of the District of Western Darfur.

The Fur are probably autochthonous to the district, with the Jebel Marra Mountain as their core area (cf. map on p. 60). Their language is only remotely related to other languages in the Sudan savannah belt (Greenberg 1966). They are sedentary hoe cultivators relying mainly on subsistence cultivation of millet in the rainy season. Residentially they are divided into villages of varying size, from about fifty to a few thousand inhabitants. In total population they probably number about half a million.

Their territory borders in the east and west on the territories of other sedentary ethnic groups (Masalit, Tama, Berti, Birgid and Daju are the most important). To the north is the area of nomadic and semi-nomadic tribes (Beni Hussein Baggara, Zaghawa cattle and camel nomads and various Arabic camel driving tribes) and to the south there are several Baggara tribes (Taisha, Beni Helba, and Rizeigat).

Before colonial administration (established in Darfur 1916) a Fur sultan ruled the Fur and at times also neighbouring groups. Today the Sudan government maintains peace in the area. A shallow hierarchy of Fur chiefs is incorporated in the Sudan administrative system. They are delegated administrative functions (collection of taxes and jurisdiction) and their decisions are sanctioned by the central government (Barth 1964c).

The historical origin of the Baggara is connected with the Arabic invasion of Sudan from the fourteenth century onwards. The Baggara claim descent from the Arabic invaders and consider themselves Arabs. While they have remained culturally distinct from earlier inhabitants of negro stock, they can today hardly be distinguished from this population on the basis of physical features.

The Baggara are cattle nomads, but most of them also practise some millet cultivation in the rainy season. They are divided into several tribal groups, each with a recognized homeland *(dar)* and with a hierarchy of chiefs. Their area extends in a belt from the Nile to Lake Chad. The Baggara local communities are migratory camps of two to twenty tents. In the rainy season they stay in their *dar* where conditions are favourable for the cattle. As the dry season approaches, lack of water and grass forces them to migrate to other areas (Cunnison 1966).

About 30,000 Baggara nomads (mainly members of the Beni Hussein and Beni Helba tribes) spend the dry season among the Fur in the lower parts of the Western Darfur. Competition for resources is slight since the two groups exploit different ecological niches. In the rainy season, when the Fur do most of their cultivation, the presence of flies and leeches makes the area unfavourable for cattle and thus also for the Baggara. Conflict does arise when cows invade dry season irrigated gardens, but this is not very important since irrigated agriculture is still only pursued on a small scale.

Ethnic categories and inter-ethnic relations

The Fur and Baggara have remained culturally distinct although they have been in contact for centuries. They differ with regard to general style of life, subsistence pattern, overt cultural features like language, house type and weapons, and standards for evaluation of performance.

Fur-Baggara contact is regulated by shared codification of the reciprocal statuses that are appropriate for members of the two groups respectively. Both the Fur and the Baggara are Muslims and may thus interact on ritual occasions. A Baggara may camp in the Fur area in the dry season, but is then subject to the jurisdiction of the local Fur chief *(sheikh* or *omda)*. In the market place they provide complementary goods: the Baggara supply milk and livestock, and the Fur supply agricultural products of which millet is of major importance to the Baggara. The herding contract is another basis for Fur-Baggara transactions. Persons in Fur villages may own cattle, but ecological conditions make it risky to keep them in the villages in the Fur area in the rainy season. Cattle-owning Fur farmers may avoid this problem

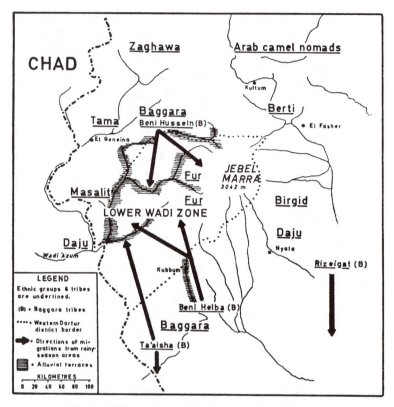

District of Western Darfur : Distribution of major ethnic groups.

by handing their cows over to Baggara nomads. The Baggara keeps the cows in his own herd and drives them to his *dar* in the rainy season. He gets the milk from the cows while the owner gets the calves. The Baggara is not responsible if predatory animals or disease kill the cows.

The articulation of Fur and Baggara is thus mainly based on the complementarity of goods and services connected with their different subsistence patterns. They agree on the codes and values that apply to the situations in which they articulate, whereas comprehensive differences are maintained in other sectors of activity. These differences do not just relate to features that are of differential functional value in the pursuit of agriculture and animal husbandry respectively, but are of a more arbitrary character like language, standards relating to kinship and marriage, and the importance of hospitality.

I shall argue here that these differences are maintained because Fur and Baggara are categories in terms of which actors identify themselves and their partners. Interaction is structured by a categorical dichotomization of people who are like oneself, with whom one may have relations covering all sectors of activity, and people who are different from oneself, having different evaluations, with whom one only interacts in a limited number of capacities. These identities are signalized by several easily identifiable features: villages of huts made of mud and straw versus camps of mat tents arranged in a circle, Fur language versus Arabic, the throwing-spear versus the Baggara lance. I shall argue that this dichotomization of ethnic identities implies restrictions on interaction and that these restrictions are crucial in maintaining the cultural distinctiveness of the Fur and the Baggara, because it allows inter-ethnic relations to cover only a small sector of activity. Differences in codes and values applying to other sectors of activity are not made relevant to inter-ethnic encounters, and consequently they are not adjusted. It is generally accepted by both the Fur and the Baggara that a person's behaviour should be judged according to the standards of evaluation that apply to *his* ethnic group.

Processes of identity change

The two groups are recruited not only by biological reproduction, but also by the incorporation of people from other groups. In the following I shall analyse the determinants by which individuals are sloughed off from the Fur local community and incorporated into a Baggara community. I shall try to show how these processes can be explained as a result of the specific character of the Fur economic system and the ecological restrictions on cattle husbandry in Darfur.

The economic system will be described here as a set of alternative strategies for the allocation of value. Such an approach focuses on the economic units, the forms of value they allocate, and the institutional mechanisms by which values in various forms may be transformed to other forms.

Among the Fur every adult individual, male or female, is an economic unit.[1] The marriage contract does not establish a family household; husband and wife thus constitute two management units. They have usufruct rights to separate fields, they plan their production separately, they keep the product in separate stores and they allocate the product independently. The only reciprocal economic commitments that the marriage contract establishes are the wife's duty to make porridge and beer for the husband (of millet taken from his store) and the husband's duty to buy clothes for his wife and children once a year. The wife is responsible for growing millet to feed the children.

Every person who is recognized as a member of a Fur local community has access to land. Land is administrated by the local chief and is allocated to members of the community according to need. Usufruct rights can be exercised only as long as one cultivates the land. When land is laid fallow after a few years' cultivation, the farmer has no rights to it any longer; rights to reallocation revert to the chief. The farmer has no right to alienate his land.

Each adult individual among the Fur has the necessary resources for a farming enterprise: access to land and his own working capacity. The management of these resources is relatively simple. The larger part of agricultural production is oriented towards the cultivation of crops for private consumption. Millet is the staple crop and is consumed in the form of beer and porridge which are the main items in the Fur diet. Several institutional rules constitute limitations and possibilities for transformations of value through the process of exchange. The sale of porridge and beer for cash is restricted by ideas of shame associated with such transactions. The institution of the beer-party does, however, allow for an exchange of beer for labour. By providing beer, one can invite neighbours to drink and help weed the millet fields. The institution of the market place allows for cash exchanges of agricultural products (onion, tomatoes, okra, chili, millet, mango, citrus), animal products (livestock, meat, milk), the blacksmith's products, and imported goods (sugar, tea, salt, cloth). The character of land-rights makes it impossible to exchange money for land. Exchange of money for labour is also restricted, since it is considered shameful to work for money. The bride price institution allows for conversion of value from the cash sector to a wife. Money is furthermore convertible into social esteem if it is spent on pilgrimage (haj) or feast (karama).

It is within these institutional rules that a Fur has to manage his resources in order to satisfy his consumption needs.

The alternative strategies of value-transformations that are possible within this framework are depicted in the diagram.

This is a multicentric system where there are restrictions on transformation of value from some forms to other forms. Some forms of

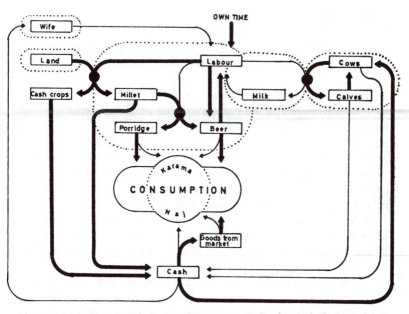

Diagrams showing the principal allocative choices open to the Fur farmers in the Lower Wadi.
Thick arrows indicate the main direction of flow ; dotted lines separate spheres of the economy.

value are thus not reciprocally convertible. One implication of this is
that they are not made comparable to each other, i.e. one has no conception of their relative value. In this system there are only two investment possibilities. One may grow millet, brew beer and invite to a
beer-party and thereby mobilize labour. Decreasing efficiency of labour
in bigger beer-parties limits the profitability of investment in this
sector. The other investment possibility is cattle. Cattle constitute the
only way of accumulating capital and are an investment that gives
profit in the form of calves. The profitability of this mode of investment is, among other things, dependent upon how the cows thrive in
the area where they are kept in the rainy season. Most Fur farmers
therefore prefer to leave their cows with a Baggara. This, however,
is also a hazardous arrangement, because it is difficult for the Fur
farmer to know whether losses stem from causes for which the Baggara
herdsman is not responsible, or whether the herdsman has slaughtered
and sold the owner's stock. The more capital a Fur has invested in
cattle, the more concerned will he be about the risk he takes when

handing over his cows to the Baggara. Five cows represent a value of about £40-50, a considerable amount of money. The Fur farmer's dilemma is that, on the one hand, the cows do not thrive in the farm-land area, but that, on the other hand, the herding contract is a risky venture.

The solution which cattle-owning farmers frequently choose when they have from five to ten cows is to establish themselves as nomads (Haaland 1968). This seems to be a paradoxical choice: the most wealthy farmers become the most marginal nomads. As nomads they will not be able to maintain the level of consumption (in terms of their evaluation of consumption goods) that they could as farmers. I will argue that the rationality of the choice can be understood when it is related to the multicentric character of the economic system.

By being a member of a local community, a villager automatically has the right to usufruct of land. A Fur has, therefore, no conception of the value of land relative to other forms of value. The choice between being a farmer and becoming a nomad is thus not a choice of whether to accumulate capital in the form of land or in the form of cattle. The choice is whether to secure the cattle capital by becom-ing a nomad one-self and living with the reduced level of consump-tion that this implies, or to continue as a farmer with a satisfying level of consumption and take the risk of losing the capital one has accumu-lated. When the cattle capital reaches £40-50 the Fur finds the first alternative preferable.

In choosing seasonal migrations the nomadic novice has to consider what conditions will be like for the cattle in various areas as well as for millet cultivation. The smaller the herd, the more heavily cultiva-tion opportunities are weighed. The income from a herd of five to ten cows is still so small that the nomad will, to a large extent, be depen-dent on millet cultivation. This implies that he cannot migrate to the Baggara land in the rainy season, because conditions for millet culti-vation are not good enough there. The Fur nomads migrate to higher, sandy parts of the Fur area where the risk of losing the cattle is smaller than on the low-lying farmlands, and where the conditions for millet cultivation are better than in the Baggara area. If the herd increases the nomad can take the welfare of his cattle more into account when he makes his choice of migrations. When he has about twenty-five cows he does not have to rely on millet cultivation, and he therefore chooses to migrate to the Baggara area in the rainy season. A successful economic career among the Fur thus starts in the village and leads to nomadic migrations within the Fur area, and finally ends up with the long rainy season migrations to the Baggara area.

In the first phase of nomadization, the Fur nomad camps together with other marginal nomads from his own area. Due to the differential growth of the various herds of the camp, disagreements about migrations may easily arise. A critical situation emerges when a herdowner has enough cattle to migrate out of the Fur area in the rainy season. If he starts the long migrations, he will have to leave the camp of Fur-speaking nomads and try to attach himself to a camp of Arabic speaking Baggara nomads. His children will then grow up learning Arabic, not Fur, and they will eventually get spouses from the Baggara communities. Each year about one per cent of the population of the lower-lying areas of Western Darfur leave the villages and establish themselves as nomads. Although those who do not succeed will return to a sedentary life in the villages where they are accepted as members, some will manage to build up herds of considerable size, and their descendants will not learn the Fur culture. They will constitute disappearing lines in local Fur genealogies.

Through the nomadization process individuals are thus sloughed off from Fur local communities and eventually incorporated into Baggara communities. But at what point does the change of identity actually take place. When does a Fur become a Baggara? Is it when he establishes himself as a nomad? Is it when he has enough cattle to attach himself to Baggara camp? Or is the ethnic transformation process completed only with his children, who have not learned Fur culture and who are not recognized as members of any Fur community? To solve this problem I find it necessary to specify the nature of ethnic identity change and the criteria applied in ethnic classification. Are we to study this as a long-lasting process of personality change and concentrate on the socializing mechanisms? Should we look at the cultural inventory of the nomads and compare it to that of the sedentary Fur and that of the Baggara, or should we try to discover how people categorize the nomadized Fur and what the crucial criteria for categorization are? I shall discuss these problems by a further analysis of some consequences of this nomadization.

I have claimed that the identities of Fur and Baggara are associated with different value standards. Some of these differences relate to the evaluation of goods and activities associated with a sedentary versus a nomadic style of life, where Fur preferences are for village-life and Baggara preferences are for nomadism, respectively. If a Fur, however, succeeds in accumulating cattle, he will sooner or later realize that the optimal way of maintaining this form of value is to establish himself as a nomad. This choice implies that he puts himself into a position where he will not have access to other values current among the Fur. According to Fur standards of evaluation, the consumption pattern of the nomad is a poor substitute for the consumption pattern of the villager: 'Milk yesterday, milk today, milk tomorrow, that is not good', complained one newly established nomad. The implication was that beer was preferable, but as a nomad he could not afford it. Unfavourable comments on the small tent that is used by the nomads, as compared to the larger and more comfortable hut of the sedentary Fur, are also frequently heard from nomadized Fur. The nomad will furthermore not have the opportunity to participate in communal activities like village dances, beer-parties and other feasts. These are the hardships faced by a Fur when he chooses nomadization. If he specializes in maximizing one form of value, cattle, his satisfaction in other goods is reduced. Judged according to Fur standards a nomad is more successful than villagers with regard to accumulation of wealth, but the activities he has to perform as a nomad clearly imply disadvantages compared with village life. An evaluation of the advantages and disadvantages of nomadic life according to Fur standards can thus not give a conclusive answer to the problem of whether a nomad will maintain his allegiance to these standards or whether he will prefer to assume Baggara identity and be judged according to the standards of that culture.

The total life situation in the nomad camp is, however, radically different from that of the village. As a nomad a person's interest is focused on cattle, the resource on which his livelihood depends, and this form of capital requires a kind of foresight in management that is not present among the sedentary Fur farmers. A subsistence based on animal husbandry thus generates a different attitude towards saving and investment. The more corporate character of the nomad family also gives a basis for long-term planning that is not present in the atomistically organized village community where the individuals' need for achieving recognition of social identity leads them to orientate a great deal of their activity towards participation in informal community life. These are circumstances that generate differences of evaluation between nomads and settled people. Do we conclude then that the value changes that are generated by the practice of nomadic subsistence will sooner or later make it impossible for a nomad to maintain his allegiance to Fur standards of evaluation? Comparative material from other ethnographic contexts suggests that the answer is no. Such circumstances do not invariably lead to a change of identity. There are ethnic groups that maintain their unity despite the fact that their populations are distributed over niches that imply just as radical differences in life situation as that between sedentary and nomadic Fur. Arabic nomads, farmers and townsmen is one such case. However, a Fur who has established himself as a nomad exhibits several socio-cultural traits that make him distinct from sedentary Fur. As farmers, husband and wife constitute separate households, as nomads they pool their resources and establish a family household similar to the household form of the Baggara. With respect to the relationship between marriage partners, there seems to be greater similarity between the nomadized Fur and the Baggara than between nomadized and sedentary Fur. But are we permitted to present social forms of that order as criteria for classification of persons as Fur or Baggara? If so, the family form of the nomadized Fur would indicate that they must be classified as Baggara when they establish themselves as nomads. Such a point of view would have to be based on a hypothesis that the similarities in social forms are a consequence of the Fur adopting Baggara ideas about the marriage relationship. I would argue, however, that this change in family form can be more adequately explained by an alternative hypothesis that does not take cultural borrowing into account (Barth 1968, Haaland 1968). Cattle nomadism implies organizational problems that make the Fur pattern of individual households inadequate. Cattle have to be herded and milked, milk has to be churned and marketed, new pastures and camp sites have to be located, and millet has to be cultivated in the rainy season. Several of these activities have to be performed simultaneously. The economic units practising cattle husbandry can therefore not be built on single individuals; they have to be built on units that include at least two persons. While the Fur value husband-wife autonomy in economic life, there is no prohibition on cooperation. As long as the family subsists by millet cultivation there is no great economic advantage gained by pooling resources; it makes no difference for the result of production if husband and wife work together or separately.

When a Fur establishes himself as a nomad, he bases his subsistence on a more complex process of production. Great economic advantages are obtained if the spouses agree on a division of labour within a joint economic enterprise. The emergence of family households among the nomadized Fur can be explained, then, by the mutual advantages secured by the pooling of resources; i.e. family households would have emerged whether there were Baggara nomads present or not. Overt similarities in social forms can thus not be used as criteria for ethnic classification if these similarities are generated by the restricting effects of ecologic conditions.

Observing a camp of nomadized Fur we notice few visible criteria by which it can be distinguished from a Baggara camp. The tents are made of the same kind of straw mats, and are arranged in the same circular pattern as in Baggara camps. The personnel of the camp use the same kind of material equipment as do the Baggara. There are thus no diacritica that signal an identity different from the Baggara (but they are easily distinguished from recently immigrated Fulani nomads). It is only when one recognizes that the language used in daily conversation is Fur and not Arabic that one can identify their Fur origin. When asked what tribe (Arabic: *gabila*) they belong to, the nomads will identify themselves as Fur. In fact, I first became aware of the existence of nomadized Fur when one of my informants in a village inquired whether I wanted to visit Fur people who live as nomads.

By their inventory of objective cultural traits, these nomadized Fur therefore can neither be classified unambiguously as Fur nor as Baggara. They seem to be persons in an intermediate position exhibiting traits associated with both of these ethnic groups, and if these traits are the basis for classification one is led to see them as constituting a transitional category. Are they then identified by themselves and by others as belonging to such a category? I have said that they identify themselves as Fur when asked about their tribe. But this does not imply that 'Fur' is their actual label, the category that defines their position in situations of contact with Fur or Baggara. If one asks a Baggara what his tribe is, he will not say he is a Baggara, but will identify himself as a member of one of the many Baggara tribes such as Rizeigat, and Beni Helba. In this context the term 'Fur' is of the same order as 'Rizeigat' or 'Beni Helba'. It is a name referring to the ancestry of the person. A Fur nomad could not have identified himself as Rizeigat because too many people would have known that his father was a Fur. The fact that the term Fur is applied to a nomad in this context does not necessarily imply that social situations in which he participates are structured by the codes and values applying to a person of Fur identity. This is the crucial criterion of ethnic classification if we approach ethnicity as a principle of social organization, as a categorization defining what can be made relevant in interaction between persons of the same and persons of different ethnic identity. From this point of view the nomadized Fur will be classified as Fur, Baggara or a separate category depending on how their participation in social situations is defined, what status sets are mobilized, and what standards are applied in judging their role performance.

As a nomad, a Fur offers the same prestations as a Baggara in transactions with members of the sedentary population. Market-like situations are defined by the same status sets whether a nomadized Fur or a Baggara interacts with the settled Fur. He will, furthermore, have the same kinds of conflicts with the sedentary Fur as the Baggara have, because of the problems involved in keeping the cows away from the irrigated gardens. But these are again similarities that arise from the practice of animal husbandry and not from sharing the same ethnic identity.

As distinct ethnic groups the Fur and the Baggara have different preferences and they accept the fact that their behaviour is not judged by the same standards. The way actors (Fur and Baggara) categorize a nomadized Fur will then be manifest in the standards they apply when they judge his behaviour.

If the nomadized Fur were judged by the standards of Fur culture, one would expect role differences to emerge between them and the Baggara. One would furthermore expect that their Fur identity would be signalized by easily visible cultural features. This, however, is, as I have said, not the case: the origin of the Fur nomads can be discovered only from the persistence of such habits as are difficult to change overnight, like language. Sociologically significant differences in role play can hardly be distinguished. This indicates that nomadized Fur are subject to the same role restraints as the Baggara, i.e. they are categorized as if they were Baggara and their performance is judged by the standards of Baggara culture. This was once clearly brought out by comments exchanged between my assistant (a Fur) and one of my informants from a Fur village community when we had visited a camp of newly established Fur nomads. When visiting a Baggara camp one expects to be received with a show of hospitality; tea is brought forth and served generously. The situation is not tense, for the Baggara act with confidence towards strangers and conversation is easy. In a Fur community there are similar idioms of hospitality, but strangers are not received in the same confident way. The Fur are suspicious towards people they do not know, and it usually takes them some time to overcome their reluctance to engage in conversation. There is thus qualitative difference between the Fur and the Baggara in situations where a show of hospitality is expected. When we came to the camp of the Fur nomads we were received in a manner resembling more the expected reception in a Fur village than in a Baggara camp. Tea was not brought forth, conversation was difficult, and a bowl of milk was served only after some time. On our way back to the village my two companions complained about the behaviour of the nomads: 'This was not the way one should be received by a nomad.' In other words, they evaluated the performance of the nomadized Fur with reference to the Baggara's standards of hospitality and not with reference to their own Fur standards.

This exemplifies, I shall argue, the crucial point in the categorical dichotomization of Fur and Baggara: a person who pursues a nomadic subsistence is categorized as a Baggara, i.e. he is expected to behave like a Baggara and he is judged as if he were a Baggara. That he speaks Fur only implies that his interaction with the farmers can be easier. Nomadized Fur still have relatives in the village community, but the kinship relations are not mobilized as often as they were formerly, and kinship status is only made relevant in a limited sector of interaction with the related villagers. The fact that nomadization is not an irreversible choice (the nomadized Fur will still be accepted as member of a local community, if he wants to turn farmer again) does not contradict this statement. The nomadized Fur has a resource that the Baggara does not have, but this it not a resource that he can exploit as a nomad, nor does it have to be maintained by any kind of prestation to the local community. It derives simply from his knowledge of Fur culture and does not affect any of his activities as a nomad. That some of the nomads have a background which makes it easier for them to return to the local community if they fail as nomads does not alter the fact that they are considered Baggara as long as they practise nomadism.

If one approaches the problem of how to classify the nomadized Fur from the social point of view, through the categories held by the actors, the difficulties of classification are solved. According to this perspective, a Fur becomes a Baggara as soon as he establishes himself as a nomad. People categorize him as Baggara, and his participation in social situations is therefore prescribed by the same rules as those which apply to members of Baggara tribes. By this approach one avoids the psychological problems involved in considering change of ethnic identity as a question of personality adjustments. Of course these problems are important and interesting, but I argue that one can most adequately study the organizational consequences of ethnic categorization when the psychological constitution of the actors is excluded from the analysis. The fact that a Fur does not change his personality immediately when he establishes himself as nomad and that he, in some situations, is not able to act like a Baggara does not alter the fact that the adequacy of his role performance is judged by Baggara standards. The social constraints imposed on him are of the same kind as those imposed on a Baggara, but he may be less able to make a successful performance within these constraints.

Nomadized Fur may therefore be regarded by other Baggara as inferior, but this means that they are inferior as Baggara, not that they are an inferior ethnic group. The inclusion of successful Fur nomads in Baggara camps and their marriages with members of Baggara tribes are facts that validate this assertion.

Thus the maintenance of the boundary between the Fur and the Baggara is probably related to the distribution of rights in productive resources. Right to utilize land accrues to everybody who is accepted as a member of a Fur village. Agricultural land is held only as long as it is actually cultivated. Access to grazing is free for those who have cattle to herd. Consequently, a person can control the factors of production only by practising the activities involved in the processes of production. The activities of farming and of cattle husbandry imply two different styles of life, and these styles are categorized as Fur and Baggara. Land and grazing rights can thus not be accumulated by any specific transaction. Only by practising activities that identify him as Fur or Baggara can a person acquire access to these resources.

Conclusion

I have tried to show the determinants underlying the nomadization of sedentary Fur hoe cultivators, and I have argued that this nomadization implies a change of ethnic identity. This analysis has been focused on conditions as they can be observed today, and I have said nothing about the time perspective of this process. I have argued that given the specific economic structure of the Fur, and given the ecological setting of the lowlands of Western Darfur, a nomadization of some Fur will follow. Both of these factors may be assumed to have been fairly constant for centuries, thus suggesting that this process has had some permanence over time.

One circumstance that I have taken as given in the analysis is the political situation. In situations characterized by inter-ethnic tension and warfare, the restrictions on change of identity would be radically different from what they are in the present situation where peace is maintained by the central administration, as the case has been since 1916. It is therefore not possible to project the rates of nomadization to periods when political conditions may have been different. I have, however, information about cases of nomadization that date back to the time before colonial rule, a fact that shows that nomadization also occurred in politically more unstable periods in the history of Darfur.

Hence, I will hypothesize that there has been some nomadization of the sedentary hoe cultivators ever since the arrival of the Arabs in Darfur, although at varying rates. Before that time cattle may have been kept in favourably located villages, but nomadism was probably not practiced as a technique of husbandry.

Certain linguistic data point to the same conclusion: Fur words for those aspects of cattle husbandry that are connected with nomadism are clearly derived from Arabic, whereas the vocabulary for describing the animal itself is Fur.

In the future, this trend towards nomadization will probably stop. I have related nomadization to the lack of investment objects in traditional Fur economy. Today, changes are taking place which alter these circumstances (Barth 1967b, Haaland 1968). Both land and labour are being monetized, a process that opens new investment alternatives for the actors. In the two villages in my field sample which have progressed furthest in the direction of a comprehensive market economy, no cases of nomadization have occurred over the last 25 years.

The nomadization trend has important consequences for the demographic balance between Fur and Baggara. The Baggara is a group that probably cannot maintain its present numerical size by biological reproduction. Two processes tend to reduce their population: sedentarization and low fertility rate. I am not able to specify any rate of sedentarization, but there is evidence of Baggara nomads settling, mainly in towns and rural areas elsewhere. The Baggara who settle are mainly those who have not succeeded in maintaining the minimum number of cattle needed in order to pursue a nomadic subsistence.

My data do not allow any assessment of the fertility rate of the

Baggara. The composition of families in the camps I visited, however, gives an impression of low fertility. That this generally may be the case among the Baggara is supported by information indicating prevalence of venereal disease (El Hadi El Nagar & T. Baashar 1962). In this essay I have described a process of recruitment to the Baggara population through the penetration of an ethnic boundary by individuals and elementary families. This process, involving the nomadization of sedentary hoe cultivators, is in fact not unique for the Fur; it also takes place among the other sedentary ethnic groups of Darfur (Haaland 1968) and it probably has an even wider occurrence in the Sudan savannah belt. The organizing effect of ethnic dichotomizations is clearly demonstrated by the fact that this nomadization process does not lead to the emergence of nomadic sections of the groups in question, but to the replenishment of the Baggara.

[1] For a more detailed documentation and analysis of the Fur economic system, see Barth (1967 a).

Ethnic and Cultural Differentiation

by Jan-Petter Blom

The purpose of this paper is to discuss the cultural and organizational requirements for the establishment of ethnic boundaries. I shall present a case in which the cultural diversification of a peasant population within a national state is shown to reflect continuous processes of adaptation to shifting circumstances in the natural and social environment. Socially, the situation is one in which the resultant differentiation presupposes symbiotic interdependencies of people in dissimilar adaptational positions and is thus reminiscent of the so-called plural society (Furnivall 1948).

However, although stereotypes and prejudices referring to categorizations of observed cultural differences are frequently held, they are never made directly relevant to the relationships between people with dissimilar backgrounds and ways of life.

Consequently, ethnic homogeneity is maintained throughout the area in spite of the apparent diversity in behavioural styles and forms of social organization. My case is thus a negative one, and through the analysis I shall try to show that the organization of ethnic identities does not depend on cultural diversity *per se,* as generally assumed in anthropology, but rather on the assignment of particular social meanings to a limited set of acts.

There is within the South Norwegian peasantry a population characterized by direct dependence upon the utilization of the high mountain environment for hunting, fishing and the grazing of livestock. This population, collectively referred to as mountain peasants *(fjellbønder),* lives in local communities which are situated in deep, narrow river valleys and lake basins close to the central high mountain plateaus.[1] These run from northeast to southwest and adjoin four major regions (see map on page 75): the eastern region (Østlandet) with farm-

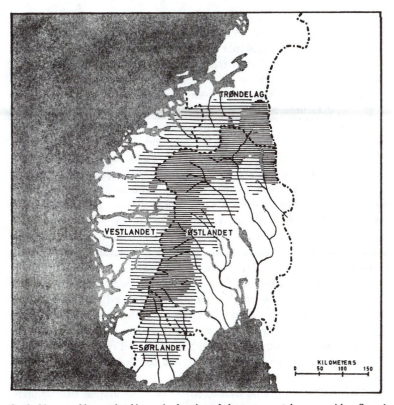

South Norway. Narrow hatching: the location of the true mountain communities. Spaced hatching: the adjacent area of central valley and inner fiordal communities with somewhat similar adaptational features.

ing or combined farming/timbering; the southern region (Sørlandet) with smaller farming/timbering areas inland and farmer/fishermen on the coast; the western region (Vestlandet) with farming populations in the interior fiord areas and farmer/fishermen on the coast; and finally the northern region (Trøndelag) with rich agricultural areas which are similar to the eastern region. Normally Norwegian farming is mixed, combining the raising of livestock and the cultivation of grain and root crops. The relative importance of these sectors depends on ecologic conditions and therefore varies regionally.

As the map shows, the main concentration of the high mountain communities is found in the eastern area at altitudes between 500–1000 m. The winters are severe and the summers short (about three months) and cool, with middle temperatures for July varying locally from 8–12° C. The landscape takes its character from the close juxtaposition of valley and mountain. An ecologic cline extends visibly with increasing altitude from open coniferous forest through mountain birch forest to high mountain vegetation such as heather and lichen. Due to the prevalence of metamorphic rock over the area, the woodland floor, as well as the mountain slopes and plains, are rich in grass, which provides excellent summer pastures. Topographically the conditions vary: some valleys are quite narrow with steep sides, others are relatively open with more broken terrain. The local communities or districts are split up into clusters of adjoining farms *(grender)*, which crowd together whenever the valley bottom or lower slopes provide small strips of arable land. Such settlements are found mostly on moraine soils away from the valley bottoms, preferably on the north or east sides where the danger of frost is least.

In regard to opportunities for farming, there is naturally a marked ecological barrier between this mountain area and the surrounding low valleys, plains and fiordal districts. In contrast to lowland farming areas, the mountain communities are located above or near the boundary for the guaranteed ripening of grain and root crops. Furthermore, even where the arable land allows for the cultivation of such crops, it is nowhere sufficient to support the population. The 'mountaineers' may therefore be characterized as a population of marginal farmers who are almost completely dependent on livestock for a living and whose in-fields are, for a large part, cultivated meadows producing only hay.

Archaeological and historical sources indicate that this area was not settled by agriculturalists until the lowland was filled. After the Black Death (1349) most of the high valleys were completely or partially depopulated, either as a direct result of the Black Death or because the people moved down to the lowlands to take possession of farms or tenant contracts which were vacant after the ravages of the plague. It was not until the sixteenth and seventeenth centuries that the high valleys again reached their former population level. Later they became greatly over-populated in the course of the eighteenth and nineteenth centuries, until the pressure was relieved by emigration to America and by later industrial development.

It is therefore reasonable to assume that the whole southern Norwegian farming population, mountaineers and lowlanders alike, has a common cultural source. On the other hand, this population has developed divergent cultural traits, or styles of life, in response to adaptive requirements and opportunities provided by variations in ecological conditions. While the lowland peasant is tied to the farm and lives a stable and regular life, the mountain peasant's adaptation is based on the exploitation of large areas. He is constantly on the move, trekking across the mountains; he is a hunter and a stock buyer. As a result the mountaineer is often attributed a certain type of character: he is a gambler, an artist and a ruffian in contrast to the sturdy, mild lowlander.

However, if we want to demonstrate the validity of the ecological approach to the problem of cultural diversification, we must be able to make a model which shows the synchronic processes that generate these empirical forms from a common cultural basis.

Since the high valleys are mainly dependent on livestock, the size of the capital (cattle, sheep, goats) of a management unit is dependent on the amount of fodder which can be acquired in the course of the short harvest season. In the traditional system of production, where the high quality of summer grazing is utilized by spring calving, haying comes in the peak season of the dairy work. This situation prevents the full utilization of the household's labour in haying. Such labour becomes men's work, since the women are able to participate only when they are free from the demands of caring for the livestock and dairying.

Moreover, as the arable patches in the high valleys are steep and stony, cultivation is labour consuming, much more so than in the lowland where it is possible to apply more efficient techniques.

Because of the density of population relative to the amount of arable land, farms are on the average too small to utilize fully the available labour potential for cultivation and likewise too small to provide a surplus of dairy products. Many peasants are therefore forced to collect fodder from the forest and natural meadows, a technique which requires a considerably larger investment of labour than does the harvesting of arable fields.

Since these resources are available in practically unlimited quantities, one can safely say that the work input in collecting fodder represents the minimal factor in this production.

While a three generation family with small children, or a two generation family with grown and half grown children, has a surplus of labour for the year as a whole, it has too little labour potential at harvest time to enable it to collect fodder for flocks that would be large enough to exploit completely the rich summer pastures. Nor would it be realistic to base production on the import of seasonal labour, since there is no easily tapped supply of labour at this season; moreover, such labour is too expensive in relation to expected profit. A significant augmentation of the household through the incorporation of additional adult members is therefore neither a feasible nor an attractive alternative.

Considering the labour potential available throughout the year, and the large resources of pasturage which the mountain peasants control *de jure* or *de facto*, it becomes clear that available productive capital is the limiting factor in increasing the rate of utilization. The most adequate adaptation would be one that made possible the acquisition of seasonal capital, in the form of livestock, during the period when pastures are available.

This situation has long been, and continues to be, a major determinant for productive activity in the high valleys. The mountain peasants have solved the problem by importing livestock from the lowlands. This is done by several institutionalized arrangements:

1. Mountaineers establish agreements with lowlanders for the seasonal rental of livestock, primarily cows and goats, thereby increasing milk production in the summer.
2. Mountaineers buy up lowland calves in the spring for fattening; these are sold in the autumn.
3. Mountaineers rent out mountain areas for the pasturing of sheep or horses.

These solutions may be combined in various ways depending on the resources of the individual farm unit, i.e. pasturage and labour.

Lowlanders also find such arrangements attractive, for a number of reasons:

1. It saves labour.
2. It supplements inadequate lowland pastures.
3. It improves the quality of the stock, since mountain pasturage is, especially for sheep, of considerably higher quality than lowland pasturage.
4. This demand for capital makes it possible to utilize otherwise

unexploited resources, such as winter pasturage on islands and peninsulas along the west coast. By renting out or selling livestock, peasants in such areas can keep herds larger than the household alone could manage to make productive, even through intensive utilization.

In this way, the mountain peasants' demand for capital has caused many lowlanders to grasp this opportunity for basing their system of production upon a symbiotic relationship. The specific details of contracts differ regionally and historically, reflecting the varying tactical advantages of the partners, but they are all founded on the unalterable ecologic contrast between the high valleys and the lowland farming areas adjoining them.

The contracts are, as far as the mountain peasant is concerned, based on three conditions: availability of abundant pastures in the summer season, an external market for seasonal rental or buying of livestock, and an external market for sale of surplus animal products. The resultant pattern of utilization of resources contributes to make the mountain farmers culturally distinctive in regard both to the type of work they do and to the specific organizational solutions which are embraced by individual households and local communities. Moreover, these circumstances not only imply specialized techniques and skills, but also contribute to the development of a characteristic mountaineer style of life, with correlates on the level of attitude and world view.

A successful adaptation presupposes the solution of a number of special technical and organizational problems. The stock must be moved to the pastures early in the summer and back to the owner or to the markets in the fall. Before the road system was sufficiently well developed for truck transport, the animals were driven long distances up the valleys or over the mountains and ferried by boat in the fiordal areas. Driving livestock was very risky, especially the crossing of high mountains in the autumn and early spring, because of unseasonal cold and snow storms. However, different types of cooperation between households made transport more efficient and reduced the risk. Cooperative agreements were also made concerning the marketing of cheese and meat. These are the basis for more recent joint efforts such as the building of proper roads to summer dairy (seter) areas, joint motorized transport of milk to main roads leading to dairies in the towns or cities, and the founding of smaller, local cheese dairies. Even so, this kind of farming carries a great deal of economic risk.

for the individual unit. On the other hand, it also involves the possibility of growth through net investments in the enterprise. This is achieved through purchase of more or better pasturage or through seasonal buying and selling of yearlings. A successful enterprise entails geographical mobility and the ability, as well as the possibility to exploit the changing opportunities in the market. This picture of the mountaineer as a gambler is corroborated by his activities as reindeer hunter and travelling middleman *(skreppekar)*. The mountain communities also tend to be the main areas for the recruitment of artist craftsmen and musicians, who sell their output or expertise over wide areas.

The foregoing analysis has attempted to show the ecological and social bases for a cultural situation which in many important respects is reminiscent of poly-ethnic societies, i.e. culturally differentiated regional populations in symbiotic interdependence based on the exploitation of different ecologic niches. However, in a poly-ethnic context, the interaction of the representatives of the discrete units observes and maintains boundaries since all, by their actions, will emphasize their respective ethnic identities — and thereby their mutual cultural differences — in such a way that their relationship is restricted to impersonal or role-specific forms. However, there is no empirical evidence to support an assertion that interaction between these mountain farmers and lowlanders is based on dichotomization of such generalized, ethnic character. On the contrary, one finds that the cultural difference is *under*communicated (Goffman 1959) by the parties to the transaction: they display the same values and utilize common idioms which stress similarity and mutual trust. Their interaction is therefore in principle identical with that which obtains between individuals within a local community or district when they are engaged in similar transactions.

These findings take us to our starting point, i.e. the question of social meanings implied by cultural diversification. The question suggests an analytical dichotomy between culture, in the sense of standards of evaluation and their codification in social categories and statuses, and culture in the sense of the manifest forms generated by such values under specific ecologic and social conditions (Barth 1966, 1968).

Consequently, if we wish to explain, on this basis, the growth and maintenance of the specialized forms of activity in the high valleys and the traditions that are established as a result, we must be able to point to an intention on the part of this population to realize ideals concerning their way of life which are common to Norwegians, or at least to the whole agricultural population.

This can be demonstrated through an examination of the way in which the mountain peasant allocates his annual production. Taking into consideration the market price for his produce, and the amount of money he needs to invest in the farm, he reserves some of his products for private consumption while income from the sale of the remainder is used to buy imports, such as flour or grain, coffee, sugar, household equipment, and some farm implements. Depending in this way on the success of his various enterprises, it is possible for a mountain peasant to achieve a consumption profile which corresponds to that of the lowlander. This is shown to some extent in the everyday diet but more importantly through the stress which is placed on conspicuous consumption, as in housing and hospitality. Optimally a part of the profit is saved either as movable property or money. This capital is transferred to the children as inheritance or dowry and serves as compensation to those who do not inherit land. In this way the child who inherits the farm, normally the eldest son, may be given the complete holding without prejudicing the position of his siblings.

It is therefore safe to say that the mountain peasants not only recognize the general criteria of rank which apply to the wider society, but that by striving to live up to the standards of the richest and most powerful people in the larger society — particularly those of the peasants who constitute their natural reference group — they also struggle to achieve the highest possible rank both within the local community and beyond it. A farmer's claim to rank is perhaps most clearly shown in situations of hospitality, since this situation gives the most dependable result in the form of social recognition. Large amounts of food are stored for this purpose, often at the expense of daily consumption. In the case of the mountain peasant, this often means that he and his family may have to restrict themselves quite drastically to achieve adequate visible advancement in the social sphere.

My analysis thus indicates that the more a mountaineer involves himself in social competition with peasants of the lowlands, and through them with most Norwegians, the more his overt style of living must diverge from that of people in other tactical positions. Through this specialization, distinctive regional cultures emerge; but the process of diversification depends on the operation of factors that militate against the systematization of cultural differences in the form of ethnic boundaries. Confronted by specific ecologic and social limitations, the mountain peasant tries to maximize ideals which, if he is successful in his enterprise, will substantially raise his rank despite his natural handicap; thus a situation arises which sometimes generates great differences in rank within the local community in the high valleys. A more concrete result of wealth and higher rank is often that one or more of a mountain peasant's children marry heirs to better farms, either locally or in lower areas, or are launched into other types of careers in the society at large. In rare cases a mountain peasant may even himself manage to transform his resources and his wealth into a reasonably good farm outside the high valley area.

Most of the mountain communities, especially in the years after the last World War, have changed considerably. The extension of the national road net crossing the area, construction of dams in connection with hydro-electric enterprises, the growth of tourism and the possibility of local industrial development have given the mountain peasant alternative productive uses for his time and local resources. The same factors which previously favoured a growing cultural diversification between regions now make a reintegration possible through urbanization.

Aspects of the analysis above are reminiscent of studies such as that of Sahlins (1958), who shows that the variation in the forms of social stratification in Polynesia can be understood as adaptive variability from a single cultural source. Historically, the argument implies the geographic expansion of a population with an identical cultural background and further implies processes of adaptation to particular local environments that offer unique possibilities for the development of patterns of leadership and inequality.

In a similar analytical tradition Arensberg (1963) shows that the peoples of the Old World are set off from all others by a unique cultural complex characterized by a food base of bread, milk, and meat · associated with a particular ecological pattern of mixed agriculture on clean-cropped fields. This adaptation is based on a cycle of land use rotating from hard field grains for bread to grassland fodder for hoofed animals, which, in turn, provide manure for the fields and consumption goods such as meat and milk, hide and wool. However, variable natural circumstances throughout the area modify this com-

plex, causing significant variations on the level of economic organization from patterns of simple subsistence to forms of specialization and
market exchange.

Being more or less in the culture area tradition, as developed by
Kroeber (1939), this 'phylogenetic' perspective on culture diversification and change might demonstrate a perfect merger of cultural and
ethnic boundaries for some areas (as is the case for Polynesia) and
considerable overlap for others. Thus the cultural-natural regions of
Europe as generated through Arensberg's approach to the problems
of diversification seem to be ethnically irrelevant for most areas. However, apart from the total empirical picture, it is always possible to
point at some kind of co-variation between the distribution of ethnic
groups and cultural features. My quarrel is consequently not with the
empirical pictures established through this procedure, but with their
assumed explanatory value for the existence of ethnic groups and
boundaries. As long as a study only shows co-variations of ethnic and
cultural boundaries, one can only make tautologies about the interdependencies between variables.

My case has demonstrated that the existence, between regional populations, of considerable cultural differences which provide a basis for
symbiotic complementarity and ample material for regional stereotypes
and distinctions, yet do not in themselves entail a social organization
of activity based on ethnic units. As already mentioned, we have to
add a further dimension, that of the social codification of some of
these cultural differences into contrastive total identities, in order to
produce ethnic groups; and this does not spring from the cultural contrast *per se*.

Against this some might argue that whenever, for example, a co-
variation of language and ethnic boundaries is emphasized, this implies
the hypothesis that language barriers are instrumental in generating
the ethnic picture. Recent socio-linguistic findings, however
(Gumperz 1958, Blom & Gumperz 1968), suggest that significant
differences in speech between various kinds of groups that are in
frequent contact are not in themselves responsible for the establishment
and maintenance of social boundaries. These differences rather *reflect*
features of social organization through a process of social codification, and thus serve as idioms of identification with particular group
values, whether sanctioned internally or forced upon the group by
outsiders.

As a final illustration of my point it may be instructive to contrast the highland-lowland relationship as described above with the relations that obtain between Norwegians and certain nomadic pariah groups such as Gypsies and Gypsy-like tramps *(sigøynere, tatere,* or *fant)* (Sundt 1850–65, Barth 1955). Like the mountain peasants and other specialized groups, these pariahs utilize specific niches in the countryside and are thereby bound in symbiotic dependence to other occupational categories — partly because they are willing to do low ranking jobs, and partly because they have a near monopoly on some forms of trade and handicrafts. In contrast to the mountain peasants they *over*communicate their cultural peculiarities during contact; they show disrespect for the standards of the peasant and especially for his criteria of rank, and their behaviour is often arrogant and provocative. Within the sedentary population their very nomadism is construed as a denial of the peasant's basic values. As a result they are distrusted, feared, and even persecuted, but they are also admired for their autonomy and recklessness; this ambivalence is expressed in a series of folk legends and songs. Interaction between Norwegians and members of these groups is therefore built on differential treatment within the frame of a clear complementarity of identities.

It should therefore be evident that ethnic boundaries do not depend on cultural differences on the level of form, but rather on culture at a more fundamental level, i.e. specific codification of these differences into complimentary statuses which differentiate a population into reference groups, supported by a charter of distinctive origins for each. The reason for the existence of such organizations must therefore be sought in the social processes which allow an initial and natural fear and suspicion against strangers to be systematized into ethnic statuses. These are social categories which provide obligatory standards for judging the behaviour of self and others and which, consequently, organize a whole range of activities into stereotyped clusters of meaning.

---

[1] The primary data on which this study is based were collected by the author in 1962 in the south-western part of the area concerned. A more detailed presentation of the material will be published elsewhere.

To test the general validity of the set of hypotheses generated through my analysis of these data, various works by folklorists, geographers and historians have been used, the more important of which are: Eskeland, A.: *Effektiviteten av ulike driftsformer i fjellbygdene,* Norges Landbruksøkonomiske Institutt, Særmelding nr. 2, 1953; Cabouret, M.: La transhumance du mouton dans le sud-ouest de la Norvège, *Norsk Geografisk Tidsskrift,* 1967; Isachsen, F.: Uvdølenes skreppehandel og driftetrafikk, *Norsk Geografisk Tidsskrift,* 1930; Reinton, S.: *Sæterbruket i Noreg,* I—III

ISFK, Oslo 1955—61; Skappel, S.: Træk av det norske kvægbrugs historie 1660—1814, *T.f.d.n. landbr.*, 1903; Sømme, A.: *Geography of Norwegian Agriculture*, Skrifter fra Norges Handelshøyskole, Bergen 1949; Østberg, Kr.: *Norsk Bonderett*, I—XII, Oslo 1914—39.

The anthropological field investigations was financed by the Registration Service of Norwegian Archeological Museums.

Dichotomization and Integration

Aspects of inter-ethnic relations in Southern Ethiopia

by Karl Eric Knutsson

This paper presents ethnographical material on ethnic groups and ethno-dynamics in Southern Ethiopia. Because of the highly varied pattern of inter-ethnic relations in this area I shall sketch the situation in two different parts of Ethiopian Gallaland. By contrasting and comparing two different sets of ethnic boundaries and their maintenance I hope to avoid giving too one-sided a picture. I also hope that this approach will make it possible to discuss aspects of boundary dynamics, and thereby contribute to a more general discussion of the problem of ethnicity.

The setting

The setting for ethnic relations that Ethiopia represents is indeed complex. In the northern and central parts of the country, there have existed during millenia kingdoms loosely organized into an Abyssinian Empire. Borders between these petty states were not very stable and the struggle to achieve imperial dominance and control over the vast Abyssinian conglomerate was continuous. In general the borders between states or chiefdoms seem to have coincided with the boundaries separating major ethnic groups inhabiting the Abyssinian plateau.

Before the conquests by Emperor Menelik during the end of the last century through which Amhara/Tigre Abyssinia expanded into the much larger Ethiopia of the present day, the central states were surrounded by a number of independent tribal groups representing a broad spectrum of organization, from anarchic segmentary structures to centralized states such as Kaffa. Into these areas where conflicts and tribal wars were endemic, Menelik and his generals brought the 'pax amharica' which set the stage for new forms of inter-ethnic contacts and relations. Increased inter-group mobility, immigration from the conquerors' ethnic groups, introduction of the victors', system

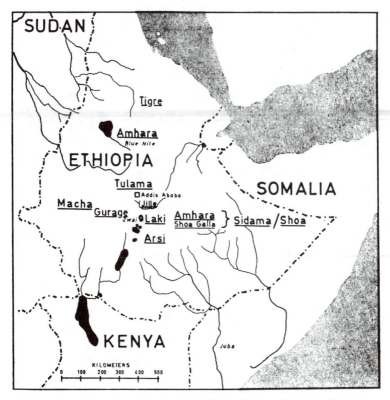

*Main ethnic groups and sub-groups in Ethiopia. Dichotomization indicated for
Amhara/Shoa Galla.*

of ethnic classification and valuation were incidents and circumstances
contributing to the present ethnic situation in Southern Ethiopia.

In many ways the setting is similar to that which was brought about
by colonialization in other parts of East Africa. There are, however,
important differences which invalidate a simple comparison. Time
has contributed to an integration of the new areas into the Ethiopian
nation in a way that was never achieved between colonizers and
colonized in other parts of Africa. It is true that the new rulers
recognized ethnic boundaries as did the European colonial powers;
the administrative division into sub-provinces and districts is principally built upon such a recognition. It is also true that elements of

indirect rule can be found, especially during the early days following the incorporation of the new territories into Ethiopia. But for the most part, Amharic control was of a more direct nature and did not therefore necessarily emphasize and strengthen tribal and ethnic identity, as was often the case under British rule further south.

Another important difference between the colonial African and the Ethiopian situation is that, although the influx of people from the Northern parts of Ethiopia was large, the immigration did not produce the ethnic and social cleavages which exist between European settlers and native Africans. The immigrants from the north were for the most part forced to live basically the same life and accept the same standard as the indigenous ethnic groups.

However, in some instances, the new rulers' policy to ethiopianize, which was tantamount to amharize, the subject groups in order to facilitate integration often had the opposite effect: ethnic identities became emphasized and polarization on ethnic grounds was increased. Thus Amharic administration produced results similar to those observed in areas under British control.

The present forms of ethnic boundaries in Southern Ethiopia have been generated within existing systems of inter-ethnic relations through processes of this kind. In the following I shall concentrate on two sets of such boundaries; those between the Rift Valley Arsi Galla and their neighbours and the ones existing in a market village among the Macha Galla in the western part of the Shoa province.

The Rift Valley Arsi and their neighbours

The Rift Valley Arsi are members of the large Arsi Galla tribal group which makes up the dominant part of the population of the Arussi and Bali provinces. Until the last generation the Arsi, who now inhabit the eastern shores of Lake Zwai and the adjoining dry savannah, lived in an area of complete Galla dominance. They subsisted on a transhumance pastoral economy that took them to the highlands around Mt. Chilalo in the dry season and down to the Rift valley plains in the wet season. Their only routine inter-ethnic contacts were with the Laki islanders in Lake Zwai — a remnant from earlier Abyssinian settlements during pre-Galla periods. With the Amharic conquest during the first decade of the present century the picture changed radically. Veteran Amhara and Shoa-Galla soldiers in the armies of Menelik were given land on the Arussi plateau. Moving into the highland in great numbers they soon reduced and finally prohibited the transhumance of the pastoral Arsi-Galla. Being deprived of one of the basic prerequisites for their ecological adaptation the Rift valley Arsi in the Zwai area turned to a crude type of maize and sorghum farming to compensate for the losses inflicted on their cattle economy. As they had little previous agricultural experience and as the Rift valley climate necessitates either irrigation or technically sophisticated dry farming, the Arsi experienced a rapid pauperization. These changes coincided with major changes in their tribal organization whereby the importance of the cohesion-creating *gada* system declined and the ritual changed from a traditional to an Islamized pattern — possibly as a protest against the Christian conquerors.

These developments set the scene for the inter-ethnic relations between the Arsi of today and their neighbours. As is clearly demonstrated even by this very brief exposé, the character of the Arsi ecological adaptation, their economy, and their political and cultural life have undergone dramatic changes during a relatively short time. In other words the Arsi of yesterday would not have had much in common with the Arsi of today. Consequently a study of their cultural inventory would not help us understand the maintenance of an Arsi ethnic identity over generations. I shall therefore only include a minimum of information on the way of life of the Rift valley Arsi, and concentrate on the description of neighbour contacts in order to indicate the nature of ethnic interaction and the mechanisms of boundary maintenance in the area.

The Rift valley Arsi of today live in clusters of 5 to 15 homesteads, inhabited by minimal lineages or segments thereof, on the dry acacia savannah surrounding the Rift valley lakes. The normal homestead is that of a polygynous household with three or four houses and a cattle kraal fenced in by thorny acacia. Despite the recent adaptation of maize and sorghum farming on some roughly cleared fields close to the homesteads they still remain basically a cattle people. Part of the herds use the still extensive areas of the clanlands between the shores of Lake Zwai and the slopes towards the highland not yet cultivated by the highland farmers. These herds are tended by the unmarried men of the homestead under the leadership of some of the senior men. Milch cows, calves, and young animals are kept close to the homestead in order to provide milk and occasionally meat for the remainder of the family.

Local political organization exhibits two dominant components: one of government administration represented on the lower levels by subdistrict governors and officially appointed local judges; the other of local leadership furnished by groups of genealogically senior clansmen, famous arbiters, descendants of former warleaders made hereditary nobles, so-called *balabatts,* by the administration (cf. Knutsson 1967), and *kallus,* ritual specialists claiming to perpetuate traditional tribal religion and self-made sheiks. In many parts of southern Ethiopia articulation between these two decision systems is poor. But this is not the case in the Rift valley Arsi communities. In part because of reluctance on the part of the central administration to keep their own officials in a potentially dangerous area in the lowlands, local leaders are often appointed to administrative posts on the subdistrict level.

Ethnic identity for the Arsi is intimately connected with the total way of life on their dry, dusty and overgrazed plains. The few who leave their cattle or those who have lost them and move into towns are no longer regarded as 'real' Arsi. They have sold or lost the part of their identity that derived from participation in Arsi life, although they still retain their Arsi genealogical charters. In other areas of Southern Ethiopia, especially in communities where inter-ethnic contacts belong to the daily routine, the display of ethnic identity is either restricted to certain sectors of interaction or determined by specific individual or group strategies. Not so among the Arsi of the plain. Here ethnic identity is continuously overtly expressed in what both Arsi and their neighbours perceive as distinct forms of organization, customs, and symbols. However, neither the Arsi nor the outsider are able to attribute the identity to any specific element or factor. To be an Arsi is to be born one, to be brought up like one, and live like one. The realization of this represents an extra reason to abstain from any attempt to map the whole inventory of Arsi culture and to concentrate on the problems of inter-ethnic contacts.

Arsi and Laki.

The interaction between the Rift valley Arsi and the Laki islanders in Lake Zwai presents most of the characteristics of a symbiotic interrelation. Some generations ago the Laki inhabited and cultivated large portions of land on the eastern and southern shores of the lake. Extensive traditions tell about fierce fighting between the Arsi and the Laki over the control of the shore land. This district was of vital importance to both groups, to the Laki as agricultural land from which they could supplement the limited produce of their island terraces; to the Arsi for pastures and free access to the water for their cattle. Eventually the Arsi succeeded in their raids and the Laki had to withdraw to their islands. Today they are almost exclusively confined to the islands of Tadecca, Tullu Guddu, and Fulduro, the only exception being some hundred who live in a few clusters on the eastern and southern shores of Lake Zwai. These latter have been able to return to the old Laki shore territory only by completely adopting the Arsi mixed cattle and agriculture economy and by conforming closely to the Arsi style of life. The Laki on the islands subsist on fishing and the meagre crops of their eroded and overcultivated terraces. Without their skills as weavers and cloth traders survival on their overpopulated stony islands would be difficult.

With the Arsi fully in control of the disputed shore-land, competition between the two groups has faded away and one finds instead today the kind of symbiotic interrelation that can be expected between two ethnic groups occupying distinct ecological niches. The islanders supply cloth, fish, and some items of merchandise and the Arsi market butter, ghee, fresh cheese, sorghum, corn, and occasionally meat. Of especial interest is the increasing Laki sale or barter of fish, which is caught in abundance in the shallow lake. All pastoral Galla as well as their Sidamo neighbours observe a strong taboo against eating fish. Fish was traditionally classified in the same general category as hippopotamus and regarded as unclean food. With the breakdown of the transhumant system and the increasing shortage of food, the taboo on fish has been weakened among the Rift valley Arsi, especially among those close to the Zwai, who now consume fish quite regularly. They do not, however, do any of the fishing themselves. This is left to the Laki with their sophisticated technique of net-throwing from small papyrus canoes.

Rift valley Arsi and the highland farmers.
The Amhara and the Shoa Galla of the Arussi highland are plough farmers exploiting the same ecological niche with identical techniques. They are members of the same, mainly immigrant, local communities. In spite of their ethnically distinct origins they share a basically common value system dominated by Orthodox Christianity. Differences between the two groups are articulated mainly in language and family structure, and to some extent in land tenure and rituals. Thus the Shoa Galla group tends towards bilingualism whereas the Amhara cling

to the exclusive use of Amharic; the Shoa Galla families are polygynous where feasible, in contrast to the monogamy of the Amharas.
The Amhara adhere strictly to the rules of the Orthodox church while
the ritual life of the Shoa Galla exhibits a dual pattern of both
Orthodox Christianity and ecstatic tribal cults led by the *kallus*.
Another characteristic of this Amhara-Galla society is the presence of
the general Ethiopian system of ethnic stratification, which in its turn
depends on differential control of such assets as administrative
authority, land, and access to the highly valued clerical knowledge of
the Orthodox church. According to this traditional stratification the
Amhara both ascribe to themselves and are ascribed by the Shoa Galla
a higher rank than other groups in the highland community.

Despite this intra-community differentiation the Rift valley Arsi
lump the highland immigrants together in one big category, referring
to them either as Sidama (the Arsi word for Amhara) or as Shoa
(people from Shoa). Although the highland Galla farmers do not
identify themselves as Amhara in intercommunication with the Rift
people, they certainly dichotomize the lowland cattle people from
themselves and act towards them as do the Amhara. I therefore argue
that the boundary that exists between the highland community as a
whole and the Rift valley Arsi is the major one relevant to a discussion
of ethnic interrelations.

The main feature of the interrelation described here is that of
Highland superiority and Arsi inferiority. Most clearly this is seen
in the two groups' competition over land. As indicated, the Arsi
pastoral type of land utilization has been displaced in the higher
zones by an agricultural technique and economy, the introduction of
which was made easy by the oscillatory nature of the former. The
only strategies for ecological readjustment that are left to the Arsi are
either sedentarization in the threatened areas or withdrawal to the as
yet uncultivated tracts which are today mostly areas where cultivation
without irrigation is impossible or close to impossible. There is also a
third course which has been tried. It consists of a compromise strategy
whereby part of a lineage settles in the neighbourhood of the highland
pole of their former transhumant territory, while the rest of the group
keeps a more mobile base at the bottom of the Rift. In some cases this
has made it possible to retain some transhumant mobility or to resort
to it during emergency situations.

Reviewing the ethnic interrelations between the Rift valley Arsi
and the highland farmers we do not find a boundary comparable to

the ecological boundary between the Arsi and the Laki. Instead the basic mechanism of ethnic differentiation is found in the different technologies of land use, and the different efficiency of these for retaining or expanding control over land. The ensuing competition has increased the dichotomization of ethnic groups to a degree which has made open conflicts common. Because of the dominance of the highland group and especially because of the support it enjoys from the Amhara-dominated administration, open defence of the traditionally pastoral areas by the Rift valley Arsi has not proved a satisfying strategy. Violent resistance being ruled out, adaptation has taken either of the two main forms described, dividing the present Rift valley Arsi into two economically distinct groups: highland type farmers on the slopes of the Rift, and savannah cattle herdsmen suffering a progressive pauperization.

As can be expected there are significant differences between both expression and maintenance of the ethnic identity between these two groups. Among the Arsi farmers on the slopes of the Rift one finds a more or less complete assimilation into the technological and economic system introduced by the highland immigrants, although many of the Arsi farmers cooperate with their lowland kinsmen in the cattle sector of their economy. However, even if the explicit aim of their new economic strategies is to become as much as possible like the highland immigrants and even if overt expression of their ethnic affiliation in dress and symbols is reduced, an Arsi ethnic identity is still fiercely maintained. This cannot be achieved in the traditional way, as this would imply retaining the whole pattern of their former pastoral life. Instead it is done by the transition to a Moslem or rather semi-Moslem system of knowledge, values and symbols that makes it possible in a partly assimilated situation to maintain and perpetuate ethnic dichotomization. This change provides an especially efficient mechanism for polarization since the very core of the immigrant Amhara ethnic identity has always been their Orthodox Christianity. Thus in contrast to the process that made Baggara nomads out of Fur farmers, the transition of Arsi cattle herdsmen to Amhara-like farmers has not made them Amhara. Instead the boundary maintaining mechanism is transferred to another sector of their socio-cultural universe.

Rift valley Arsi and the Jille.
The Rift valley Arsi have as their northern neighbours the Jille, who belong to the Tulama tribal cluster among the Galla, and who strongly

deny any genealogical relationship with the Arsi, although both groups agree that they are Galla. Like the Arsi, the Jille live on the Rift slopes and bottom. They are not so pre-eminently a 'cattle' people as Arsi, but have traditionally subsisted on a mixed economy of poor maize, millet, and sorghum farming in combination with cattle herding. They have also traditionally been more sedentary and have never adopted transhumance. They are the only northern Galla who still have a functioning moiety system and they have also, more fiercely perhaps than the rest of the Tulama group (with the exception possibly of the Jidda), clung to their remnants of the Gada system and the rituals accompanying it. Perhaps the interrelation between the Arsi and the Jille should be classified as intertribal rather than interethnic. After all they belong to the same main tribal group and speak dialects not very remote from each other. However, the dichotomization demonstrated in their interrelation, the fact that both stress not their common but their different ancestry within the very large Galla people, and finally the fact that they exhibit fairly different systems of social organization, make it reasonable to include them in this context.

In contrast to the cases already described, the territorial boundary between the Arsi and the Jille is an absolute one following in the main the Awash river in the east-west direction and the eastern side of the Maki river in the north-south direction. In contrast also to the interaction between Arsi and both the Highlanders and the Laki, where market exchange is a prominent feature, there are few, indeed negligible, transactions of this kind between the Arsi and the Jille. This can perhaps be correlated with the fact that, in spite of other differences, the two groups exploit similar types of territories with similar techniques. The differences in technology and produce necessary for the creation of an extensive market exchange simply does not exist. The main markets in Jilleland are found in a semicircle to the north where the Jille can trade with Tulama Galla from higher zones and with immigrant Amhara, Gurage, and other groups.

Although presented here only as a sketch, the material allows a rough identification of the interrelationship between the Arsi and the Jille as one of segmentary opposition between groups striving to monopolize the same type of ecological niche. The seriousness of the competition over grazing land and plots of arable land has contributed to both the hostility and to the creation of the jealously guarded frontier. The similarities in their ecological adaptations have helped not to bridge the boundary but to strengthen it as this very similarity has precluded transactions and exchange. Thus paradoxically the geographically and 'politically' most articulated ethnic boundary in the Rift valley Arsiland obtains between the culturally most similar groups.[1]

The polyethnic market village in Macha

Any discussion of inter-ethnic relations in Southern Ethiopia's Gallaland would be incomplete if it only contained reference to a system in which ethnic groups tend to be territorial units. All over Southern Ethiopia such a situation is actually rapidly changing into one where different ethnic groups are living more or less mixed in the same areas and local communities. It is in these communities that the typical Ethiopian system of ethnic stratification can be observed.

When the rich Macha grazing and farming land was incorporated into the Ethiopian Empire during the end of the last century radical changes were brought about similar to those in highland Arussi. Traditional, segmentary rivalry between local groups was reduced and eventually completely eliminated. Intra-Macha mobility and delocalization increased and Machaland was opened up to immigration from other parts of the Empire. The Amhara established their control over local politics and administration. Veteran Amhara soldiers moved in to become landlords and farmers.

With increased mobility went the creation of market villages and the expansion of existing towns, a process that has received a tremendous impetus from the construction of roads during the past few decades. Although their *couleur locale* is influenced by the ethnic origin of the people of the region and by the surrounding landscape, these market towns have many traits in common all over Ethiopia. They represent in the midst of their traditional rural hinterland a new type of community. They serve as the administrative centres in their districts and as such house government offices and courts both frequented by crowds of people who, to the outsider, seem to be veritable addicts to the procedures of litigation.

These towns grow rapidly by the immigration or rural population from the hinterland attracted by town life and the services that can be found in the shops, bars, clinics, and schools. To this comes the influx of officials, traders, daily labourers, prostitutes, and beggars often recruited from distant areas. Together, all this has created a radically new setting for ethnic interrelations where ethnic boundaries exist in the midst of the local community. The role of ethnicity as a basis for organization consequently displays markedly different features in comparison to the situation described above where ethnic boundaries in the main coincided with territorial borders. Thus ethnic amalgamation is more pronounced in the sense that all sectors associated with decision-making and exchange are integrated. This is readily seen in the field of local politics, where any mature male member of the community may associate himself with any of the existing factions. Likewise the exchange of goods and services comprises all groups in the town.

However, a tendency for single groups monopolize certain sectors of community life is evident and overtly manifested. The administrative machinery is in the hands of predominantly Amhara officials. This is reflected in the sphere of factional politics, where the leaders are usually Amharas or big 'Amharized' Macha landlords. In the sphere of economic exchange shopkeeping is more or less monopolized by Gurage immigrants from the south-western part of the Shoa province while grain trade is predominantly in the hands of Moslem Galla immigrants from Jimma.

The system of ethnic stratification and the tendencies towards ethnic monopolization of different sectors of community life are illustrated by patterns of communication, specifically in language habits and inter-ethnic marriages.

The 'political' language is without question Amharic. All communication of an official nature, all court procedures, all discussions within the *ider* — a community association — are held in Amharic. If a significant group of the participants does not understand Amharic, translation may be arranged. Exceptions from this pattern are very rare. Even if the judge, the official communicator, or the chairman of the meeting happens to be a Galla he uses Amharic which may then be retranslated into Galla.

In trade, which forms an interaction system incorporating the great proportion of the total population of the village and its rural surroundings, choice of language is freer. But even here the system of ethnic stratification can be registered. If one of the actors in a transaction belongs to a ethnic group of higher rank, the tendency is to use, if possible, his language in intercommunication. Thus the Galla grain trader will use Amharic when discussing business with his Amhara faction leader. He will, however, speak Galla to his Galla neighbour and also Galla to the Gurage shopkeeper, whom he regards as having a 'lower' ethnic status.

The same observations are valid for the whole pattern of ethnic identification both between members of the market village who are well aware of their respective ethnic identity and between villagers and outsiders. One can also easily recognize the ambivalence towards ethnic identification associated with stratification. Thus rural Galla with knowledge of Amharic would either deny or be reluctant to accept an exclusive ethnic evaluation from any member of the market village, which, by the rural population, is regarded as an Amhara community. The same is true of ethnic demarcation between residents of the village itself where such distinctions are accepted in dealings with individuals of 'higher' ethnic status but rejected or suppressed vis-à-vis members of a 'lower' ethnic group.

The same basic features are evident in the pattern of inter-ethnic marriage. Intermarriage in the Macha market village largely constitutes a one-way traffic of women from lower ethnic groups to higher. An exception is the different pariah groups such as tanners, potters, and the like, who are strictly endogamous. A similar situation obtains for those with the lowest possible economic standard of life.

The upward transfer of women is related to the fact that a wife's ethnic background will not, or at least not seriously, affect the ethnic status of the husband, his household or his children, whereas a woman who marries a man of a lower ethnic status than herself will be downgraded, since her household and her children are classified with the husband.

Although strategies pursued by various ethnic groups in the fields of politics and economics are ethnically determined, reference to ethnic identity as such is rarely overtly expressed by the villagers in these fields of interaction. The domains where ethnicity is explicitly used as a basis for organization and as a criterion for separation and dichotomization of persons are, as I have already indicated, most prominently those of family and kinship and in part also the ritual life, notably on the level of family and small group rituals.

Thus although marriages are no longer endo-ethnic, ethnic identification and references form a significant part of any marriage preparation. But the overt expression of one's ethnic identity is found in small-scale rituals and feasts with exclusive participation of members of a single ethnic group. During the Galla neighbourhood beer-feast one can hear songs and stories about earlier independent periods. The songs are about the brave Galla warrior and his cowardly enemies, about the beautiful Galla girls, and the superiority of the Galla pastoral life that the minstrel and the audience themselves have abandoned. The same ethnically oriented up-grading and bragging can be heard in the Macha Galla *kallu* rituals, the Moslem Jimma Galla holidays, and the Gurage ritual brotherhood meetings.

So far I have emphasized trends towards ethnic monopolization within the ethnically integrated sectors of the market village life and circumscribed levels on which inter-ethnic integration is weaker and polarization tendencies consequently stronger. Simultaneously, indications of decreasing polarization and diminishing influence of ethnicity as a basis for organization are observed in the village today, particularly among the younger generation. Several conditions contribute to this new trend:

The economic basis for all the villagers is the Central Ethiopian Amhara type of agriculture or trade of agricultural products. The majority of the village males and a large minority of the females are bilingual, a fact that tends to neutralize the influence of ethnic, cultural heritage and pave the way for smoother routine interaction. The customs and habits of every day life are levelled little by little. This also applies to ethnic symbols such as cloth, hair-do and ornaments. The introduction, at least formally, of the Orthodox church and its extensive regulation of life through its fasting and ceremonial rules have also contributed to give the village community a unitary set of symbols, although integration in the ritual field is, as I have already pointed out, less marked than it might seem.

This general integration process has taken several different forms in the market village community. One which is easily observed is the Amharization strategy adopted by a Galla or Gurage who has been able to accumulate the resources needed that make such a role attractive — one must remember that to act the part of a *poor* Amhara would be of little avail since one of the basic ingredients in the Amhara ethnic status is its very connection with economic and political superiority. Amharization does not mean, however, that there is a complete change of a person's ethnic status. There is definitely a loss in his original ethnic identity. It will be said about him that he is not 'Galla any longer', he likes to be 'like Amhara'. But he will nevertheless not be accepted as Amhara either by his original group or by the Amhara. He has lost part of his ethnic identity without gaining a new one.

Another strategy is exemplified by some of the young and better educated villagers: the teachers, the health personnel etc. It consists of a conscious suppression of what the individual regards as tribal in favour of what he believes to be an Ethiopian identity. The choice of such a strategy does not, like the former, weaken the person's original ethnic identity in the eyes of his village neighbours, nor does it meet with any envy from his group of origin or opposition from any aimed at 'goal' group. It creates instead a basis for more flexible interaction with both high and low ethnic groups. In addition, although the ascription of an 'Ethiopic' ethnic identity in most of the towns and villages discussed here still mainly represents a theoretical strategy, it is being increasingly acknowledged and promoted through the expanding educational system.

Summary
This brief exposition of inter-ethnic relations and ethnic distinction in Southern Ethiopia has certainly not helped to formulate any easy answers to problems related to ethnicity. Instead it has revealed a broad spectrum of various types of ethnic boundaries, boundary maintaining mechanisms and inter-ethnic strategies. Here I shall only briefly consider a few questions posed by the material.

It seems first of all to be quite clear that any concept of ethnic group defined on the basis of 'cultural content' (e.g. Naroll 1964) will not suffice as a tool for the analysis of ethnicity in its various interactional contexts. Only when ethnic distinction, stratification, or dichotomization are part of the individual's or group's strategies for preserving or increasing control of resources social status or other values is a meaningful interpretation feasible.

Hence ethnicity becomes not one single universally applicable term but rather the representation of a wide range of inter-relations in which the dominant reference is to an ethnic status ascribed on the basis of birth, language, and socialization.

If one accepts this, a study of ethnic inter-relations becomes necessarily a study of ethnic processes: that is the emergence, continuation, and change of inter-ethnic relations. Thus several processes can be recognized in the Ethiopian material:

In the case of the Rift valley Arsi versus the Highland peoples, the tendency dominating the ethnic interaction is one of increasing polarization and dichotomization in a situation of mounting competition over productive resources. Since the interaction is between a dominant expanding highland population with a settled economy, which controls administration and access to resources on the one hand, and an originally transhumant and retreating Arsi lowland herdsman population on the other, the latter's only efficient strategy is adaptation to, and, optimally, assimilation in, the highland ethnic groups. This strategy, however, is not easily accomplished because of the vested interests of the highland groups in the potentially rich agricultural areas on the peripheries of the highland and because profitable agriculture in the lowland areas is only possible for a sophisticated plantation and irrigation agronomy.

In the East, the inter-ethnic relations between the Lake Zwai Laki and the Arsi represents on the other hand a process of weakened dichotomization in favour of symbiotic intercommunication, which can certainly be explained by the reduction in this area through Arsi dominance of the same competition over niche control and production resources which are increasing on the highland slopes in the west.

Towards the Jille no marked changes in a traditional polarized relationship can be noted. Here a territorial division and a low degree of intercommunication has continued because of the lack of the minimum prerequisites for economic exchange and potentially conflicting interests in the same ecological niche.

A fourth basic process is finally found in the Macha market village, where inter-ethnic integration is increasing in important sectors of community life, although the Ethiopian ethnic stratification model is still a decisive factor within the integrated spheres where it sometimes seems to form the very basis for the pattern of integration itself.

---

[1] I am here excluding the pariah groups of hippopotamus hunters, the Weyto, who live scattered along the shores of Lake Zwai. Although there is complete social separation between these and the Arsi, there exists economic exchange.

Ethnic Stability and Boundary Dynamics in Southern Mexico

by Henning Siverts

Problem and area

The population of Highland Chiapas in southern Mexico is aptly characterized as heterogeneous. Culturally distinct groups are in contact within the same general area, forming a composite social entity, the members of which are constantly interacting in certain spheres of life, notably in the realm of business transactions (Siverts 1965b).

We are thus confronted with a typical 'poly-ethnic society' based on economic specialization and symbiotic interdependence between the constituent units. Interaction between representatives of ethnic categories seems to be founded on a dichotomization of generalized identities, and the cultural differences are over-communicated. Transactions across categories are therefore different in principle from those in which the partners engage with people of their own kind.

Hence, Highland Chiapas may resemble the type of society which Furnivall (1944) describes as 'plural', the characteristic of which is the combination of ethnic segmentation and economic interdependence.

The present paper describes the distribution of assets and forms of interaction in the area with reference to the question of boundary maintenance. More specifically, it asks the question of why the Tzeltal-speaking Oxchuc Mayas prefer to remain Indian and largely ignore or resist national integration and westernization.

Thus the basic topic of this paper parallels Haaland's discussion of the Baggarization of the Fur (p. 58 ff.). But rather than showing how individuals of one ethnic category change their identity, I am trying to explain the circumstances which seem to discourage attempts to do so. In both instances the line of argument is tied to economic considerations; likewise the conceptual framework shows enough similarity to warrant comparison.

The basic assumption on which the analysis rests is that a 'steady

The central highlands of Chiapas (Tzeltal-Tzotzil area).
Only a few towns and pueblos are shown.

state' of the sort met in Chiapas can only be brought about when individual actors constantly face similar dilemmas of allocation of labour and capital to which the repertoire of responses is limited and stereotyped. It is further assumed that the cultural biases, which form part of the constellation of constraints, tend to be confirmed and hence perpetuated through the repeatedly rewarded choices.

The area with which we are concerned comprises the colonial-style town of San Cristóbal Las Casas[1] and its hinterland, i.e. the plateau summit of the Highland with its northern and eastern flanks of slightly lower-lying districts. The whole area covers approximately 1,000 sq. miles. Elevations range from 3,000 to 6,000 ft. Gentle slopes make human habitation easy in parts of the area, but much of it is extremely rugged, with steep slopes, sharp ridges and deep gorges.

Despite unfavourable conditions, agriculture is the main productive pursuit, with subsistence based upon the cultivation of maize and beans. Among some of the rural inhabitants animal husbandry, notably sheep-raising, is of considerable importance. The townspeople are traders, merchants, artisans, officials, and professional men. Closer inspection reveals the existence of systematic regional differences also among the rural communities. Not only are there great variations in productive activities; there are, in addition, contrasting social forms, i.e. a juxtaposition of a number of distinct ways of life.

Language habits serve to accentuate these cultural distinctions. The highlanders speak different languages and dialects. Furthermore they show great variations in styles of clothing.

Chiapanecans make use of several verbal categories in referring to these variations. A principal distinction is made between *Ladino* and *Indio*. The first term is assigned to those who speak Spanish as their main language and pursue a Spanish-derived way of life. The second label is applied to persons who speak an Indian language as their mother tongue, and who dress and 'behave as Indians'.

In its turn the word *indio* or the diminutive *indito* may elicit a list of sub-categories such as *Zinacantecos, Chamulas, Oxchuqueros, Cancuqueros,* etc. These are names given to actual groups of people, distinguished from each other in terms of particular features of dress, and the products they carry to the market of San Cristóbal Las Casas. Thus, among the Chiapanecan highlanders, the following statement is a sufficient characterization of one such category, viz. the Zinacantecos: 'Zinacantecos wear big, flat hats with coloured ribbons, white shorts, pink scarfs and sandals with tall leggings. They are salt traders and live in the municipality of Zinacantan.'

Field observations over the last 40 years leave the impression that the range and general content of these idioms are fairly constant, and that the number of people using them is increasing.[2] Census reports of the last 30 years seem to corroborate this belief:

The proportion of Indian speaking persons is stable, and in some

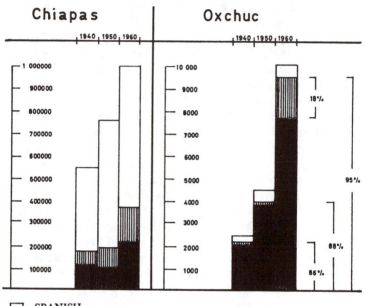

☐ SPANISH
▦ INDIAN: Bilingual
■ INDIAN: Monolingual

Proportion of Indian-speaking persons 5 years of age and older in the State of Chiapas and in the municipality of Oxchuc.
S o u r c e : Censo General 1940/1950/1960 (Estado de Chiapas), Dirección General de Estadística, México D. F. M. German Parra: Densidad de la población indígena en la República Mexicana, conforme al censo de 1940. Memorias del Instituto Nacional Indigenista, Vol. I, No. 1, México D. F., 1950.

parts of the region under study a marked increase is noted (see accompanying Table). Although the accuracy of Mexican vital statistics may be questionable for certain areas and periods, we may nevertheless trust the general trend of the reports; and if this trend reflects a social and demographic reality, our conclusion must be that the Indian speaking 'tribes' or *pueblos* maintain their populations and retain their idioms according to the stereotype established for each group of people.

Considering the long period of contact between the indigenous population and the colonists, military campaigns, epidemics, political pressure, land expropriation, and finally, the impact of the national policy of recent years to integrate the Indians in national political and economical life — we find it remarkable that assimilation is minimal and ethnic boundaries remain intact. It should be noted, however, that the notion of 'ethnic boundary' does not involve the assumption of *identical* idioms being transferred from time immemorial. Rather, the boundary implies the constancy of a set of idioms communicating minimal contrast between segments of the population. Indeed, many traits considered typically Indian today have been identified as imitations of ceremonial items and 'customs' of Spanish origin. A curious instance illustrating this is the ceremonial costumes used by the Chamulas during their *fiesta de carnaval:* Imitations of French grenadier uniforms used by Maximillian's troops in 1862 (cf. Blom 1956: 281).

Signals of identification, whatever their 'origin', serve the purpose of ascribing ethnic status to individuals, thus guiding or directing their interaction. The problem of explaining the persistence of such characteristics may consequently be approached through a study of the sectors of life where representatives of the diverse categories articulate.

In the following I shall therefore present a sketch of the forms of interaction which take place within fields or sectors of activity such as *the market* and *the administration.* Both sectors are treated as rather inclusive in this paper, i.e. education and ritual are not separated from 'administration', and the 'market' comprises various forms of business transactions.

In the process of description I will attempt an analysis which will expose an assemblage of factors sufficient to produce a situation of boundary stability. However, in order to perform the analysis, we will need to survey the form and nature of the assets which the actors can bring to bear on the situations in which Ladinos and Indians interact. Our first task, then, is to describe the distribution of resources.

Distribution of resources and productive activities

Land is a scarce resource, the ownership if which is in the hands of both Indians and Ladinos. There are principally two forms of land tenure:

1. The pastoralist ranch and cash crop plantation of the Ladinos. The property is individually owned and subject to purchase; it is exploited by means of a small number of hired hands and the labour

provided by an attached Indian community, descendants of those who originally owned the territory.

2. The collective and unalienable lands of an Indian community, or section of community, in which individual households exploit limited patches on the basis of usufruct. These lands are utilized by means of slash-and-burn cultivation of maize and beans. Labour is provided by the members of the household for most of the year. During the planting season, larger work teams are formed on the basis of kinship and friendship networks.

Regional variations in natural resources and technological skills favour the development of specialization of production. In the Indian communities part-time specialists manufacture traditional handicraft goods such as pottery (waterjars), woollen ponchos and sashes, wooden chairs, musical instruments, cordage, charcoal, firewood, and salt. These wares are brought to the market of San Cristóbal Las Casas together with the other Indian surplus produce.

Other industries, including forges, gunsmiths' shops, construction works, and a great number of small-scale industries producing Indian ceremonial paraphernalia are all exclusively Ladino; and most of these activities are confined to the town itself, which, market included, is controlled by Ladino merchants and intermediaries. The accompanying figure shows the distribution of some of these items and productive activities (p. 107).

Confrontation of assets and the sectors of articulation

Ladinos and Indians are competitors and opponents with regard to certain land areas as well as interdependent partners in an economic system where the Indians generally act as producers of agricultural products and consumers of industrial goods, while the Ladinos appear as traders and producers of industrial and handicraft wares and consumers of Indian cultivated food.

Transactions are for the most part consummated in the town of San Cristóbal Las Casas.[3] Indians carry their products to the town market and sell them directly to consumers, or, far more commonly, sell the products to Ladino merchants who resell them in the market. A prominent figure in the system of interchange of goods is that of the atajadora (interceptor), a Ladino woman intermediary who makes her living by waiting for Indians on the outskirts of the town, buying from them and then reselling the products in the market or in her shop.

At first glance there seems to be little economic justification for the

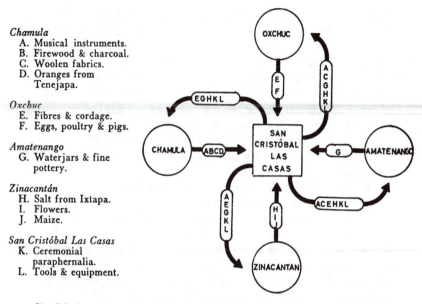

Chamula
  A. Musical instruments.
  B. Firewood & charcoal.
  C. Woolen fabrics.
  D. Oranges from
     Tenejapa.

Oxchuc
  E. Fibres & cordage.
  F. Eggs, poultry & pigs.

Amatenango
  G. Waterjars & fine
     pottery.

Zinacantán
  H. Salt from Ixtapa.
  I. Flowers.
  J. Maize.

San Cristóbal Las Casas
  K. Ceremonial
     paraphernalia.
  L. Tools & equipment.

Simplified representation of the San Cristóbal market indicating the main flow of goods.

existence of these intermediaries, since the Indians are heading for the market in any case and are likely to spend all day in town. However, the bargaining for retail sales takes more time than Indians from distant places are willing to spend. An additional reason is that the business of fractioning and haggling over prices demands certain skills including full command of the Spanish language and experience of the market. Hence the Indians prefer the rough but swift treatment by the ladies. The manner in which the *atajadoras* treat their Indian suppliers illustrates the somewhat imperious way in which Ladinos habitually behave towards Indians. The Indian is supposed to be shy and a simpleton who does not know how to trade, a belief which has the quality of a self-fulfilling prophecy. It makes it much more difficult for the Indian to deal with Ladinos on any but the most elementary commercial level. This invites harsh practice in dealings with him; neither does he possess many civil resources, save for the Office of Indian Affairs. It is likely that a considerable number of grave cases of cheating will occur before an Indian overcomes his fear of authorities and offices in order to present his complaints to them.

San Cristóbal Las Casas may be characterized as an Indian market town run by Ladinos. In the town, Indians get rid of their surplus goods in return for which they can bring back tools, and equipment of all sorts, including ceremonial paraphernalia, 'Indian clothing material', and finally, all the various handicraft wares produced by other Indian communities. The primary importance of the town is indeed as a centre of redistribution for a tremendous hinterland (cf. figure p. 107).

Characteristically, the town is divided into quarters or *barrios*, the members of which specialize in one or another activity aimed at the satisfaction of particular Indian appetites. The *barrio* of Santa Lucía is dedicated to the production of fireworks — important for any Indian *fiesta*. Another *barrio*, Cuxtitali, concentrates on buying and butchering pigs; inhabitants of that *barrio* travel as far as the jungle to the east, buying pigs ahead of the planting season, when the Indians want to get rid of their pigs to avoid the fencing in of the molesting animals. The pig-dealers also hawk cloth and trinkets during their travels. It should be added that the Indians as a rule never eat their pigs; they are raised for the single purpose of transforming maize into cash.

The market town, furthermore, is the natural seat of local administration and federal agencies, including police, a military garrison, telegraph, telephone, post office and health authorities. Of prime importance is the Labour Agency, mediating the seasonal labour demand on behalf of the big coffee plantations on the Pacific Coast. Coffee picking in the fall is the single labour offer made to the Indians from the 'outside'. Only impoverished Indians on the outskirts of town may sometimes be put to odd jobs in the garden or in the shop of a rich Ladino. Otherwise openings are non-existent for Indians simply because they are not supposed to command the sufficient skills — among them language and general education.

Thus the Ladinos control the labour market as well as the distribution of goods and services.

Except for two notable cases to the contrary (to be discussed later), Ladinos hold all positions of authority and bureaucratic offices within the regional government and administration. In the present context this includes Federal and State agencies as well as the municipal government of San Cristóbal Las Casas — an entity of the first order within the ranking system of municipalities.

The township of San Cristóbal enjoys jurisdiction over a much more extensive district than the mere municipal territory, an expression of which is the placing of Ladino secretaries in the local governments of the Indian communities, otherwise run by the native inhabitants. Normally, then, political control of the hinterland is exercised through administrative means. However, it should not be overlooked that Ladino dominance is based on military superiority and the omnipresent threat of resorting to physical force. At the slightest provocation a military detachment or police force may be ordered to garrison an Indian *pueblo*.[4] Indeed, neither the traditional tribal leaders, the *principales*, nor the subordinate body of civil-religious officers are in a favourable position to resist such a measure since their mandate is questioned by the superimposed and officially recognized municipal government, the *Ayuntamiento Constitucional*. This latter body controls the police force and therefore has effective sanctions at its disposal. However, in spite of the fact that the *Ayuntamiento* is predominantly Indian in composition, its extra-tribal sources of authority and allocated tasks tend to canalize its decision-making activities. This neutralization is reinforced and made effective through the presence of the Ladino Secretary (cf. Siverts 1960). Thus the 'old regime' of the *principales* is curtailed by the *Ayuntamiento,* and the 'new regime', in its turn, is supervised by the Ladino functionary. As long as the Ladinos are able to uphold this key position in local administration, their grip on internal politics will remain relatively firm; and the only means by which an Indian body politic could possibly replace the Ladino officer with an Indian would depend on the candidate's demonstrated ability to fulfill the requirements of the office — literacy and sufficient knowledge of the Spanish language and the business of Mexican administration.

This brings us to another important asset over which Ladinos have almost exclusive control, education. Only quite recently has it been possible for a few gifted Indians to attend secondary schools. Most Indians have no education at all, but through the educational program launched by *Instituto Nacional Indigenista*, primary schooling is now offered to children in several Indian communities.

So far, however, the lack of means and knowledge of Spanish have served as effective obstacles to Indian education and participation in professional life. Hence the Ladino dominance of the police and military forces, telephone, telegraph and the courts, implying the total control of information and coercive power on the part of the town and its inhabitants.

Since the law students are recruited from the landowning and commercial middle and upper classes of the town, loyalities toward representatives of these categories of people are much more likely to occur than some form of idealistic pro-Indian responsibility. From the Indian point of view, 'justice', is secured through kin or friendship ties between the lawyer and his clients. It is also very much a question of money. The notoriously low level of wages and salaries for civil service officers makes bribing an acknowledged, although illegal, procedure for obtaining advantageous judicial decisions. This is probably why *Asuntos Indigenas* has instituted free legal aid to Indians. However, few Indians know that such an institution exists.

Generally speaking, Ladinos consider Indians as inferior beings, or children, from whom it is proper to demand subordination and obedience. They believe that they themselves represent the 'superior culture' — another *raza* (race). Until recently only Ladinos were permitted to mount a horse, and it is still very uncommon to see Indian riders, even among the Indian horse owners. Since, however, the Indians are the producers of necessities, represent an indispensable labour force, and are the main consumers of Ladino products, efforts are made not to affront or insult the Indians unnecessarily. Therefore, in their daily dealings directly with Indians, Ladino merchants, rancheros and plantation owners behave in a friendly, paternalistic manner.[5] On the other hand, they never invite Indians to their parties and *fiestas*. An exception to this rule was observed in the ceremonial centre of Oxchuc in 1962 when the Indian *presidente* of the municipal government was invited to a formal betrothal party of a prominent local Ladino; apparently the idea was to give the event an official stamp.

Intermarriage between Ladinos and Indians is likewise exceptional and looked upon with great disgust. A Chanalero (Indian) teacher residing in Tenango married a poor Ladino woman, but although the family as such enjoyed the prestige of the husband's office, neither Ladinos nor Indians accepted them as Ladinos.

This brings us to a related but quite separate issue, viz., instances of change of identity, (cf. p. 101). In the highland setting, strikingly few cases of 'passing' are on record, which is not surprising considering that change of identity, by its very nature, is a matter of an individual's or family's hidden past. Nevertheless, poor townspeople are sometimes referred to as *revistidos* — 'those who have changed clothes' — by their fellows a little better off. Fragments of life histories reveal that Ladinization[6] is a social reality. There is a constant seepage into the city of the unsuccessful from a small number of Indian communities to the south and east of San Cristóbal Las Casas. A typical case is P . . . . from Aguacatenango who was deserted by her Chanalero husband; she claimed that no alternative solution existed but to move to town with her two children to look for servant jobs. Similarly, orphaned children are sometimes taken care of by a Ladino family. They will grow up in a Ladino environment, eventually to be acknowledged as 'semi-civilized'. It takes at least two generations to get rid of the stigma of Indianhood.

Passing the ethnic barrier, then, requires a complete transposition, involving the abandonment of home, family and whole way of life. Commonly the decision to 'become a Ladino' is a desperate measure, the only way out when everything else seems to fail. The decision to move away and take up residence in town automatically involves a precarious livelihood in the urban slum at the bottom of the social ladder. Ladinization means leaving behind an existence in an egalitarian society to pick up the humblest status in a stratified one.

However, at least two well-known cases of successful passing may be cited. Indeed, 'passing' may not be an adequate term since the cases referred to involve Chamula Indians who managed to maintain a double identity. They built personal careers on the basis of extensive business enterprises in Ladino society while openly presenting themselves as Chamulas.

Their choices of business were of such a nature that the Indians generally considered their activities beneficial to them. The most spectacular of these entrepreneurs, the late Erasto Urbina, established a hardware store to meet the Indian need for cheap tools. Urbina spoke Tzotzil, and he did not cheat his customers, who consequently preferred to deal with him rather than expose themselves to the bad treatment by the Ladino shopkeepers. Thus his business grew, and his power kept pace with the growth of the firm. He was even elected *presidente* of San Cristóbal Las Casas and married into a prominent Ladino family.

But Erasto Urbina exemplifies the possible outcome of skilled manipulation with assets which most Indians do not have. For the majority, the Ladino world is dangerous. In the Indian *pueblo* of

San Bartolomé they narrate the myth that the Ladinos were created from the horses' excrement while the Indians are *bac'il winik* (true men). In the foreign, Ladino setting, the Indians assume a modest and subservient posture.

To summarize our description so far:

The main sectors of articulation, the market and the administration, are differently organized, serving different ends. The gross effect of both sectors is the maintenance of stereotype transactions between partners in a dominant-subordinate relationship based on ethnic criteria. As going concerns these two sectors of articulation form a framework of mutually confirming regulations for interaction. The market provides for the circulation of goods and services while the administration offers political protection of the (status quo) distribution of assets on which the market activities are based, while collecting part of the profit directly and indirectly in the form of taxes and bribes.

Such a complementarity in the actual working of the two sectors seems to be clearly related to certain basic premises in their respective organizations. One such premise is the regional autonomy derived from the Mexican Constitution, the implication of which is the development of local social forms beyond effective Federal control. Provincial administration may therefore establish rules and routines in direct response to local power constellations. In Highland Chiapas, power is shared by the plantation owners, the big merchants and the Catholic Church. The administration is furthermore largely recruited from these circles. The Indians are not represented. Except for cases like Erasto Urbina, Indians do not enter the powerful elite which runs the market and supports the administration. For the Indians, San Cristóbal Las Casas is an external site of exchange, a market *place* rather than a market for major investments and profit seeking.[7]

This observation brings us to another basic condition for the smooth operation of the market-administration constellation as a principally Ladino undertaking: the ethnically defined barriers for the free exchange of major factors of production such as land and labour, implying a negligible or non-existent participation of Indians in this sphere of transactions. In other words, local constraints on the allocation of labour and capital produce an opportunity situation which seems to prevent Indians from extra-tribal investments. By the same token, such investments can only be realized through the abandonment of tribal territory and the change of identity. However, leaving the home means renunciation of the very asset on which life is based: land. Consequently Indians may not be in favour of such a solution. This situation is most dramatically illustrated by the Oxchuc case. In the following I will therefore describe in more detail how land tenure tends to restrict Oxchuqueros in their choice of activity and hence identity.

Land tenure and its implications in Oxchuc

In the *pueblo* of Oxchuc, males are entitled to a share in the jointly owned landed estate through patrifiliation. Membership in the corporation is determined by patronymics and common residence.

In order to utilize their asset, Oxchuqueros are obliged to cultivate their allocated patches in the prescribed manner, i.e. slash-and-burn agriculture based on the staples, maize and beans. In addition they grow fruits and vegetables in small quantities (house site garden), and raise hogs and poultry for sale. The only cash grop grown is the maguey from which fibres and cordage are manufactured. Alternative enterprises seem to be discouraged by local ecological conditions as well as by cultural circumstances (or axioms of propriety and demeanour): it is improper and associated with great social costs (witchcraft and ridicule) to deviate, even in minor details, from the ordinary Oxchuquero practices of production and consumption. This has been amply illustrated by the social unrest which followed the introduction of Protestantism in the area. Protestants were likely to demonstrate their independence and 'new way of life'; and even their very moderate investments in equipment, whitewashing of houses or a variant way of sowing beans were looked upon with great scepticism, sometimes leading to witchcraft accusations and ending in homicide.

This rigidity with regard to manner of exploitation of fields on the part of the shareholders is understandable, considering the consequences of permitting free enterprises on territories which are liable to be returned for redistribution at any one time. Likewise no part of the corporate estate may be alienated by any individual member, the implication of which is that a man cannot claim compensation for leaving his share to his companions if he wants to migrate and start afresh where conditions are better. (Oxchuc is not well suited to agriculture, and the scarcity of land is a grave problem.) Thus he has no capital at his disposal with which to build a new life outside the tribal borders. Another point is that there exist no alterna-

tive places of settlement, except for certain remote resettlement areas
of dubious reputation. Nor is it possible to obtain well paid jobs outside Oxchuc which permit permanent settlement and transfer of the
family. An Oxchuc male is therefore placed in an opportunity situation
which forces him to accept the membership in his patrilineal name-
group and make use of his rights in land at the locality in which he
was born. This choice involves a number of secondary privileges and
obligations, among them the right to be treated as a full member of
the tribe, entailing a set of aspirations with regard to positions of
prestige in the hierarchy of tribal offices. This right, however, is just
an aspect of a general obligation to serve one's fellow tribesmen in
whatever capacity one's superiors see fit. Thus a tribesman is bound
to accept a nomination as ceremonial sponsor of a *fiesta* whether he
thinks he can pay the expenses involved or not. Fear of the old men's
wrath and supernatural powers keep most people in line with the
expectations.

Conclusion

One single factor, the principle of land allocation, produces a
situation which, in combination with the ecological constraints, such
as the presence of a Ladino ethnic category defending its position in
the web of transactions, tends to limit the range of activities of
individuals born as Oxchuqueros.

For a youth of Oxchuquero parents simply to disown his origin and
leave seems to be too costly to be worth the attempt. He has to live
with it, and the only way of doing it, is to accept the package deal
offered to him by his seniors: 'Stay put as Oxchuquero and reap the
fruits of your only asset, for which you renounce the major portion of
your autonomy.' His reward is a livelihood and potential power and
prestige within the Oxchuc frame of reference.

As already indicated the consumption profile is restricted by local
economy and cultural biases. It is furthermore directed by the available
offers of consumer goods in San Cristóbal Las Casas where Ladinos
encourage certain purchases while impeding others. Consequently, by
acting as an Oxchuquero, and taking upon himself both household and
ceremonial responsibilities, an individual is constantly rewarded by
tribesmen and Ladinos alike. The spheres of action and conversions,
then, in which the Oxchuquero can most profitably participate, have
the feed-back effect of confirming the very axioms on which the system

is based. Hence, idioms such as language and costume, tend continually to communicate a social and cultural distance between the groups of people which are complementary in the system of production and consumption of the Highland Chiapas social entity.

Nevertheless the number of bilingual Indians is steadily growing. Furthermore Indian teachers are operating in the Indian communities. An Indian elite is taking shape (Siverts 1964). But does this imply Ladinization? How much Spanish does a man need to know and how much education is required before he is able to make the jump?

Apparently, language training and general knowledge are not minimal factors as long as openings for this kind of expertise are limited to positions in Indian society. What education brings to Indian social life is an additional platform for political activity in a strictly Indian setting (Siverts 1965c). Hence the young elite, while boasting of their knowledge of Ladino ways, do not aspire to be accepted as Ladinos but are rather anxious to obtain recognition in their own society. And the only way by which this can be done is by converting their expertise into useful activities such as acting as interpreters and backing their fellow tribesmen in their dealings with the outside world. Thus the 'new leaders' constitute an asset for the whole community in the sense that internal administration as well as negotiations vis-à-vis the Ladinos and San Cristóbal Las Casas are made more efficient.

In return for their services, the 'experts' are given positions and sometimes material benefits in kind and in money.[8] In other words, the elite is incorporated into the community; and the Ladino education, rather than producing Ladino ideals and Ladino identity, is turned against Ladino administration and outside influence, reinforcing tribal pride and Indianhood.

But Indianhood in this context is typically confined to the tribe, one's own *pueblo*. At present there is apparently no tendency to extend the idea of Indianhood to neighbouring *pueblos* or to Mexican Indians in general.[9] On the contrary, each *pueblo* is a self-contained unit; and the tribesmen see no alternative way of dealing with people in this world except commercial interaction with Ladinos on unequal terms, and ceremonial communication and small scale trading on equal terms with other Indians at patron saint feasts.[10]

The poly-ethnic situation, then, such as is met in the Highlands of Chiapas, is strikingly different from the typical minority situation of Northern Norway, discussed by Eidheim (pp. 39 ff.). A Lapp may try to fake his identity or to live a double life as a kind of Norwegian and as a back-stage Lapp. The Indian highlander is always an Indian whether at home or interacting with Ladinos. His destiny is shaped by a situation in which his Indianhood is the very basis for interaction.

[1] Former capital of the State of Chiapas, still seat of the bishopric. It is recognized as *Cabecera de Distrito*, i. e. 'capital' of the Highland district.

[2] Cf. Blom and La Farge 1927; Blom 1956; Aguirre Beltrán 1953; Guiteras Holmes 1946; Pozas Arciniega 1948, 1959; Redfield and Villa Rojas 1939; Villa Rojas 1942—44, 1947; Cancian 1965; Vogt 1966; Siverts 1965a; Pitt-Rivers and McQuown 1964.

[3] Within the tribal border trade takes place at three levels: a) delayed exchange between close relatives and neighbours; b) trade in kind (bananas for beans) with indirect reference to Mexican currency between remote relatives and acquaintances: 50 e = 1 bundle bananas = *pulato* (pot) beans, sizes of measures varying with the season; c) ordinary exchange by means of currency between unrelated and distant living tribesmen.

[4] Cf. the case of 'calling military assistance' to Oxchuc in 1960 during a period of alleged 'unrest' (Siverts 1964: 368).

[5] It is characteristic that Ladinos always address Indians in 2nd person (plural and singular) which is otherwise insulting. The use of 2nd person plural is considered an archaism elsewhere in Mexico where the 3rd person is reserved for a non-specified plurality (of persons).

[6] The neologism Ladinization (Ladinoization) is borrowed from McQuown and Pitt-Rivers 1964.

[7] Cf. the discussion of the 'peripheral market' (Bohannan 1963: 240 ff.).

[8] Teachers receive salaries from *Instituto Nacional Indigenista*, relatives provide labour for cultivating their fields, and friends and neighbours frequently bring gifts to their households.

[9] 'Indianhood' in this sense only exists among romantic intellectuals and certain idealistic absentee politicians.

[10] Pan-Indianism is as foreign to the Oxchuquero or Cancuquero today as it was during the uprisings of yesterday, notably the great insurrection of 1712 when these two tribes temporarily joined forces in a frustrated attempt to fight the Spaniards (Pineda 1888). It is perhaps symptomatic that they lost an obvious victory because hesitation and disorganization were more prominent features of the military operations than determination and coordination; and this may serve as a dramatic expression of the poly-ethnic situation where a highly segmented majority fails to make a concerted effort at neutralizing a dominant and organized minority. But of course, the Spaniards never constituted a real minority; they represented the larger society just as the Ladinos do today.

Pathan Identity and its Maintenance

by Fredrik Barth

Pathans (Pashtuns, Pakhtuns, Afghans) constitute a large, highly self-aware ethnic group inhabiting adjoining areas of Afghanistan and West Pakistan, generally organized in a segmentary, replicating social system without centralized institutions.

A population of this size and organization, widely extended over an ecologically diverse area and in different regions in contact with other populations of diverse cultures, poses some interesting problems in the present context. Though the members of such an ethnic group may carry a firm conviction of identity, their knowledge of distant communities who claim to share this identity will be limited; and intercommunication within the ethnic group — though it forms an uninterrupted network — cannot lightly be assumed to disseminate adequate information to maintain a shared body of values and understandings through time. Thus, even if we can show that the maintenance of Pathan identity is an overt goal, for all members of the group, this will be a goal pursued within the limited perspective of highly discrepant local settings. Consequently the aggregate result will not automatically be the persistence of an undivided and distinctive, single ethnic group. How then can we account for the character and the boundaries of this unit? The following analysis attempts to answer this question by analysing and comparing the processes of boundary maintenance in different sectors of Pathan territory. Since our questions concern processes over time which have produced and sustained a pattern that we observe today, I shall concern myself with the traditional forms of organization which have predominated and still largely obtain in the area, and not with the recent process of penetration of some parts of Pathan country by modern administration.

Pathan communities exhibit a great range of cultural and social forms (see map on p. 118). (1) In a central belt of barren hills running

Pathan area: distribution of adaptational form.
Digits refer to numbers in the text pp. 117—119.

through most of the country are found villages of mixed agriculturalists, organized in egalitarian patrilineal descent segments with an
acephalous political form. (2) In favoured localities in the mountains,
and in the broader valleys and plains, more intensive agriculture is
practised, based on artificial irrigation; in these areas Pathans proper
are landowners or owner-cultivators, while part of the village population consists of tenant Tajiks (south and west) or servile tenant and
menial castes (east and north). Political forms are largely based on
the segmentary organization of the Pathan descent groups, some places
in acephalous systems, elsewhere integrated in quasi-feudal systems
within the prevailing states and increasingly subject to bureaucratic

administration. (3) Other sectors of the Pathan population live as administrators, traders, craftsmen or labourers in the towns of Afghanistan and Pakistan, as an integrated part of those two states. (4) Particularly in the south, a large sector of the ethnic group lives a pastoral nomadic life, politically organized as tribes with, in part, very great autonomy. Finally, some groups practise extensive labour or trading migrations which bring individuals and small groups periodically far outside the geographical boundaries of Pathan country.

Such diversities of life style do not appear significantly to impair the Pathans' self-image as a characteristic and distinctive ethnic unit with unambiguous social and distributional boundaries. Thus the cultural diversity which we observe between different Pathan communities, and which objectively seems to be of an order of magnitude comparable to that between any such community and neighbouring non-Pathan groups, does not provide criteria for differentiating persons in terms of ethnic identity. On the contrary, members of this society select only certain cultural traits, and make these the unambiguous criteria for ascription to the ethnic group.

Pathans appear to regard the following attributes as necessarily associated with Pathan identity (cf. Caroe 1962, Barth 1959):

1. *Patrilineal descent.* All Pathans have a common ancestor, who lived 20–25 generations ago according to accepted genealogies. Though genealogical interest is considerable, knowledge of accepted genealogies varies both regionally and individually. The acceptance of a strictly patrilineal descent criterion, however, is universal.

2. *Islam.* A Pathan must be an orthodox Moslem. The putative ancestor, Qais, lived at the time of the Prophet. He sought the Prophet out in Medina, embraced the faith, and was given the name of Abd-ur-Rashid. Thus, Pathans have no infidel past, nor do they carry in their history the blemish of defeat and forcible conversion.

3. *Pathan custom.* Finally, a Pathan is a man who lives by a body of customs which is thought of as common and distinctive to all Pathans. The Pashto language may be included under this heading — it is a necessary and diacritical feature, but in itself not sufficient: we are not dealing simply with a linguistic group. Pathans have an explicit saying: 'He is Pathan who *does* Pashto, not (merely) who *speaks* Pashto'; and 'doing' Pashto in this sense means living by a rather exacting code, in terms of which some Pashto speakers consistently fall short.

Pathan customs are imagined by the actors to be consistent with, and complementary to, Islam. Parts of this body of custom have been formalized and made overt by tribal councils and administrators as custom law, while some written and a considerable oral literature concerns itself in a normative and patriotic fashion with the distinctiveness of Pathan culture. The value orientations on which it is based emphasize male autonomy and egality, self-expression and aggressiveness in a syndrome which might be summarized under the concept of honour *(izzat)*, but which differs from the meaning that this word has been given in Mediterranean studies, in ways that will become apparent as the analysis proceeds.

Together, these characteristics may be thought of as the 'native model' (cf. Ward 1965) of the Pathan. This model provides a Pathan with a self-image, and serves him as a general canon for evaluating behaviour on the part of himself and other Pathans. It can clearly only be maintained if it provides a practicable self-image and is moderately consistent with the sanctions that are experienced in social interaction; and some arguments in my analysis of boundary-crossing will be based in this very point. However, this 'native model' need not be a truly adequate representation of empirical facts, and for our analytic purposes I believe that Pathan custom can more usefully be depicted in a few central institutions of Pathan life. These combine central value orientations, by which performance and excellence can be judged, with fora or other organizational arrangements in which the relevant behaviour can be consummated and exhibited. The analysis of boundary-maintaining processes in different parts of the Pathan area, which will be made below, requires an understanding of three such institutions which dominate three major domains of activity: *Melmastia*=hospitality, and the honourable uses of material goods, *jirga*=councils, and the honourable pursuit of public affairs, and *purdah*=seclusion, and the honourable organization of domestic life.

Hospitality involves a set of conventions whereby the person who is on home ground has obligations towards the outsider to incorporate him into the local group, temporarily be responsible for his security, and provide for his needs. The obligation is brought into play by the visitors' presenting himself in the alien setting. Accordingly, a stranger on the road who passes close to someone who is having a meal will be offered food, someone coming to a village will be greeted and helped by residents, a friend making his appearance will promptly be made welcome. In return, the guest is obligated to recognize the authority and sovereignty of the host over property and persons present. In this host-guest relation, any single encounter is temporary and the statuses thereby reversible and reciprocal, and hospitality is thus easily an idiom of equality and alliance between parties; a consistently unilateral host-guest relationship, on the other hand, entails dependence and political submission by the guest.

The appropriate forum for hospitality among Pathans varies in distinctness and scale according to local circumstances, but involves the allocation of publicly accessible space to the purpose: a special men's house, a separate guest room, or merely a place to sit. The space and occasion together may be described as a forum because they provide the opportunity to act out behaviour which can be publicly judged according to scale and quality. Specifically, it gives the host an opportunity to exhibit his competence in management, his surplus, and the reliance others place on him. More importantly, it shows the ease with which he assumes responsibility, and implies authority and assurance — basic male Pathan virtues. On a deeper level, it confirms basic premises of Pathan life: that wealth is not for amassing, but for use and is basically without importance, that only the weak man is attached to property and makes himself dependent on it, that the strong man bases his position on qualities within himself and people's recognition of these qualities, and not on control of people by the control of objects. The self-esteem of a poor hill farmer can thus be maintained in the face of the wealth and luxury of neighbouring Oriental civilizations — yet at the same time a means of converting wealth to political influence through hospitality is provided within the terms of Pathan values. While strangers are made to recognize the sovereignty of local people, local leaders can build up followings by feasting fellow villagers in a unilateral pattern. Apart from the way in which these ideas about hospitality facilitate the circulation of persons and information in anarchic territory, and protect locals from invidious comparisons with strangers, they can also further the political assimilation of servile dependents under Pathan leaders.

The *council* among Pathans is a meeting of men, called together by one or several of those present so as to arrive at a joint decision on a matter of common concern, and may thus refer to an *ad hoc* meeting or to an instituted tribunal. The matter of common interest may be a conflict between the parties present or the planning of a joint action. The relationship between members of a council is one of equals, with no speaker or leader; the equality is emphasized by circular seating on the ground and the equal right of all to speak. The body does not finalize its decision in a vote: discussion and negotiation continue until the decision is unopposed, and thereby unanimous and binding as an individual decision by each participant. A faction which will not accept a decision can only avoid commitment by leaving the circle in protest.

The council is thus a forum where important Pathan virtues, such as courage, judgement, dependability, and morality can be acted out, while a man's influence and the respect shown him is made apparent through the procedures. On the more fundamental level, this organization of councils confirms the basic integrity and autonomy of men, and the basically voluntary nature of the social contract among Pathans. It allows groups of men to arrive at joint decisions without compromising any participant's independence; it produces binding corporate decisions about concerted action without dissembling the structure of egalitarian balanced segments through the introduction of any one's right to give commands.

Finally, *seclusion* establishes an organization of activities which allows a simultaneous emphasis on virility and the primacy of male society, and prevents the realities of performance in domestic life from affecting a man's public image. Pathan value orientations contain a number of contradictions if they are to be made relevant simultaneously in behaviour before mixed audiences. Thus, the emphasis on masculinity and virility has an aspect of sexual appetite and competence — yet eagerness to indulge oneself is 'soft' and severely ridiculed. Agnatic ideology and the emphasis on virility implies a high evaluation of males and male company over females; yet it must be through the company of females that the essence of virility is consummated. Finally, there is the problem of vulnerability through 'things' and the infringement of rights. We have seen how explicit valuations of freedom and autonomy are furthered through hospitality, through the denial of attachment and importance in things. Yet male rights in women, in sisters and wives, cannot be denied and liquidated in that way: a male is dependent on, and vulnerable through, his women.

To all these contradictions, the seclusion of women and encapsulation of domestic life is an adequate behavioural solution. It also makes possible a domestic organization that allows a realistic accommodation between spouses. The sexuality, dominance, and patriarchy demanded by public male values need not be consummated in public; the primacy of male relations can be confirmed in the public sphere without any associated sexual passivity; and at the same time the interaction between spouses need not be perverted by a male performance designed for a public male audience. The resultant pattern of domestic performance is difficult to document; but its adequacy is suggested by the relative absence among Pathans of divorce or adultery murders, by the trust placed in females by nomads and migrants who absent themselves periodically from their wives, and by the traditional view of mothers and sisters as upholders of family honour, spurring their men to bravery, etc.

These three central institutions combine to provide Pathans with the organizational mechanisms whereby they can realize core Pathan values fairly successfully, given the necessary external circumstances.

They also facilitate the maintenance of shared values and identity within an acephalous and poly-segmentary population. The public fora provide opportunities to perform and be judged by other persons regardless of residence and political allegiance; they mediate judgement and public opinion over large areas. Whenever men meet in councils, wherever guests arrive and hospitality is dispensed, core Pathan values are acted out and adequacy of performance is judged and sanctioned. Thus, agreements can be confirmed and maintained and the reality of shared identity perpetuated despite the absence of any nuclear, prototype locus or example.

Moreover, the values thus realized are shared, in general terms, by surrounding peoples: success as a Pathan implies behaviour which is also admired by non-Pathans. The ethnic identity therefore remains one that is highly valued by members also in contact situations, and is retained wherever possible. An understanding of the boundary mechanisms of the Pathan ethnic unit thus depends on an understanding of the special factors that can make it untenable or unattractive to sustain this identity. These vary in different marginal areas of Pathan country, and will be discussed in turn.

The southern Pathan boundary is one where Pathan descent groups, organized politically through lineage councils, face centrally organized Baluch tribes along a clearly demarcated territorial border. This border does not coincide with any critical ecologic difference, though there is a cline from lower and drier areas in the south to slightly wetter and more mountainous country towards the north. During recent historic times, the ethnic boundary has been moving northward through the intermittent encroachment of Baluch tribes on marginal areas.

The main factors involved in this process have been analysed elsewhere (Barth 1964a) and need only be summarized briefly. The critical factor is the difference in political structure between Baluch and Pathans. Baluch tribes are based on a contract of political submission of commoners under sub-chiefs and chiefs (Pehrson 1966). This is a form that freely allows for reorganization and assimilation of personnel, and the evidence for the historical growth of Baluch tribes through confederation and individual and small group accretion is quite conclusive.[1]

Southern Pathans on the other hand are organized in localized segmentary descent groups. Though many of them have chiefs, these are headmen of descent segments from which clients are excluded; and political decisions are made through egalitarian councils. Assimilation of non-descent members can only take place through clientship under persons or sections of the tribe. It involves, for the client, an inferior, non-tribesman serf status, attractive merely as a last resort. What is more, the arrangement is not very attractive to the potential patron either, for several ecologic and social reasons. A client in this area can produce only a very limited surplus from which a patron could benefit, whereas the patron's obligations to his clients are quite comprehensive. He is not only responsible for protecting and defending him; he is also held responsible for any offence which the client may cause. And in an egalitarian society where security springs from a man's ability to rally communal support, the political advantages of controlling a few clients are very limited. Thus, whereas Baluch chiefs compete for influence and tax income by incorporating new members into the tribe, people seeking attachment are turned away from Pathan groups due to the inability of that structure to incorporate them. Any person or small group who through war, accident, or crime is torn lose from his social moorings will thus be drawn into a *Baluch* political structure. Furthermore, as centrally led units, these are more capable of pursuing long-term strategies than are the bodies of Pathans, mobilized through fusion and *ad hoc* councils; and though Baluch tribes may lose battles, they consequently tend to win wars — swelling their own ranks in the process by uprooting fragments of personnel — and thus steadily encroach on Pathan lands.

The result is a flow of personnel from Pathan groups to Baluch groups, and not vice versa. Indeed, large parts of some Baluch tribes acknowledge Pathan origin. However, the incorporation of Pathans into Baluch type political structures goes hand in hand with a loss of Pathan ethnic identity, so the categorical dichotomy of Pathan tribes and Baluch tribes remains. The reasons for this must be sought in the clash between Pathan values and political circumstances.

Naturally, participation and success in a Baluch tribe requires facility in Baluch speech and etiquette and thus a certain assimilation of Baluch culture. However, this degree of versatility and bilingualism is widely distributed and so the external situation does not seem to require a change in identity. Rather, the critical factors are connected with the actor's own choice of identification, and all bias him in the direction of Baluch identity. I have discussed how the council provides a favoured forum for Pathan political activity, which allows Pathans to act jointly without compromising their autonomy. Membership in a centrally directed Baluch tribe, on the other hand, does irrevocably compromise this autonomy: a man must make himself the dependent, the client, of a leader and cannot speak for himself in the public forum. Judged by Pathan standards, clientship places a man among the despised failures, subordinates among independent commoners. Among Baluch, on the other hand, self-respect and recognition as an honourable commoner does not require this degree of assertion and autonomy; the costs, by Baluch standards, of being the client of a chief and nobleman are very slight. Virility and competence need not be demonstrated in the forum of political councils, to which commoners have no access, but is pursued in other fields of activity. By retaining a Pathan identity in a Baluch setting, a man would run the risk of being judged by standards in terms of which his performance is a failure, while judged by the standards current in the host group his behaviour is perfectly honourable. It is hardly surprising, then, that any one assimilated has chosen to embrace the identity that makes his situation most tolerable. As a result, changes in political membership are associated with changes in ethnic identity, and the clear dichotomy of persons and tribes is maintained despite the movement of personnel. Only one small category of people forms an exception to this: a few families and segments of Pathans who have been subjected by Baluch as serfs or slaves (cf. Pehrson 1966: 12), and being the dependents of Baluch commoners cling to an identity which can at least offer them a claim to honourable origin, though no recognition among free Pathans.

The western margins of Pathan country exhibit a very different picture (cf. Ferdinand 1962). Here, the adjoining area is largely occupied by Persian-speaking Hazara, and Pathan pastoral nomads and trading nomads penetrate deep into Hazara territory and settle there in increasing numbers. This is apparently a recent situation which came about only after Amir Abd-ur-Rahman of Afghanistan defeated and subjugated the Hazara. Before that, ethnic intermixture seems to have been limited. The Hazara were a poor mixed farming population of mountaineers, organized under petty chiefs and capable of defending their territory, while the Pathans held the broad valleys and plains. The basis for this former exclusive territorialism should be sought in a combination of political and ecologic factors. As mixed farmers, the Hazara exploit both an agricultural and a pastoral niche, so both Pathan farmers and nomads constitute competitors to them. Moreover, a tribal political system of petty chieftains, as found on both sides, has very little capacity to provide for the articulation of differently organized ethnic groups in a larger system. The relationship between tribally organized Hazara and Pathan communities would thus inevitably be one of competition and mutual attempts at monopolization of resources along the border. The apparent stability of the border between them can be understood as a result of a balance between gains and losses: with the forms of political units that obtained, the costs of conquest and penetration of Hazara country by a Pathan tribe were greater than the expected returns.

The relative pacification that resulted from the incorporation of Hazarajat into the state structure of Afghanistan radically changed these circumstances. Competition in the exploitation of resources was freed from the concomitant costs of defence and penetration, and pastoral nomad Pathans started moving in seasonally to utilize the summer pastures. Moreover, greater freedom of movement has opened a niche for traders, and Pathans, with access to the sources of trade goods, have swiftly moved into this niche. Whereas trade in settled towns is somewhat despised and largely left to special, low ranking groups, the life as a trading nomad, who, heavily armed, penetrates foreign areas and takes large risks both personally and financially, is one that provides rich opportunities to demonstrate male qualities valued among Pathans. Through the institutional device of credit with security in land, these traders have not only been able to create a profitable volume of trade, but are also gaining control over agricultural land. As a result, there is a progressive trend towards settlement of Pathans as landowners among the Hazara.

This trend exemplifies a pattern of extension and ethnic co-residence which is characteristic of many Pathan areas. Pathan expansion northward and eastward, which has been taking place over a very long period, has certainly occasionally taken the form of migration and conquest with wholesale eviction of the previous population; but more frequently it has resulted in only a partial displacement of the non-Pathan autochthones. In these cases, Pathans have established themselves in stratified communities as a dominant, landholding group in a poly-ethnic system. Through much of the western area, the dichotomy is between Pashtun and Tajik, i.e. Persian-speaking serfs, while in the eastern areas, Pakhtuns are contrasted with a more highly differentiated, but largely Pashto-speaking, group of dependent castes.

One of the preconditions for these compound systems is clearly ecological. From the Pathan point of view, it is obvious that dependents will only be accepted where the disadvantages of having them, i.e. increased vulnerabilitiy, are estimated to be less than the economic and political advantages. In the barren hills of the south, I have argued that this leads to the rejection of clients. In richer agricultural areas, on the other hand, particularly where there are opportunities for artificial irrigation, farm labour produces very large surpluses so that profitable enterprises can be based on the control of land. As a result, the option of establishing oneself as a landowner and patron of others is an attractive one. Political supremacy may variously be maintained through an integration of serfs as true clients (hamsaya), or it may be based on the less committing obligations that follow from unilateral hospitality. Where surpluses are very large, this latter pattern is most common, as seen in the development of men's house feasting in the north (Barth 1959: 52 ff.); and by this means Pathans can gain political influence over dependents without very greatly increasing their own vulnerability.

Pathan identity can readily be maintained under these circumstances, since they allow an adequate performance in the various fora where such an identity is validated. However, political autonomy in the system is founded on land ownership. Long-term ethnic boundary maintenance will thus presuppose mechanisms for monopolization and retention of land on Pathan hands. Persons who lose control of land must either be given reallocated fields on the basis of descent position or else denied rights as Pathan descendants and sloughed off from the group. On the other hand, land acquisition by non-Pathans must be contained and their participation in Pathan fora prevented unless they can be fully assimilated to Pathan status.

Several patterns of this are found, among them that of Swat, where those who lose their land also lose their descent position, while Saints and others who are given land are none the less excluded from participation in council meetings or in men's house hospitality. Thus conquering Pathans are able to integrate other populations in a political and social system without assimilating them; other ethnic groups and status groups can also infiltrate the system in dependent positions where niches are available, as have pastoral Gujars or trading Parachas. However, the cultural differences that go with the Pathan identity versus dependent dichotomy clearly tend to become reduced over time. Within the whole stratified community there is a very close and multifaceted integration that furthers this trend. Most social life can be related to a religious context of dogmatic equality. There is a constant circulation of personnel through hypergamous marriages as well as loss of land and rank. Finally, there are a multitude of contexts where a fellowship of ideals and standards are made relevant to groups that cross-cut strata: in games, in hunting, in war and bravery, non-Pakhtun and Pakhtun are joined, and judged and rewarded by the same standards of manliness.[2] As a result, the whole stratified population tends to approach a uniformly Pathan style of life as well as speech. Therefore, though the local version of the ethnic name *(Pakhtun* in the case of Swat and Peshawar) continues to indicate the dominant stratum internally, it is increasingly used collectively to designate the whole population in contrast to the population of other, non-Pashto-speaking areas. In this sense, then, the internal boundary tends to lose some of its ethnic character.

The eastern margins of Pathan country, towards the rich and populous Indus plain, illustrate a different combination of some of these factors. Repeatedly through history, tribes and groups of Pathans have swept out of the hills and conquered large or small tracts of land in the Panjab or further east, establishing themselves as landlords. Yet, here it is the conquerors who have become progressively assimilated, and the limits of Pathan country have never moved far from the foothills area, except for the almost enclosed area of the Peshawar plains. The ethnodynamics of this boundary may thus be simplified as a continuous pressure and migration of personnel from the Pathan area, balanced by a continuous absorption of the migrants into the plains population, with the rates of these two processes balancing along a line at a certain distance from the foothills. The direction and rate of assimilation must be understood in terms of the opportunity situation of Pathans settled in the plains. These plains have always been under the sway of centralized governments; for purely geographical and tactical reasons they can be controlled by armies directed from the urban civilizations there. Any landholding, dominant group will therefore be forced, sooner or later, to come to terms with these centres of power, or they will be destroyed. However, Pathan landlords can only come truly to terms with such superior powers by destroying the bases for the maintenance of their own identity: the defence of honour, the corporation through acephalous councils, ultimately the individual autonomy that is the basis for Pathan self-respect. Such landlords are trapped in a social system where pursuit of Pathan virtues is consistently punished, whereas compromise, submission, and accommodation are rewarded. Under these circumstances, Pathan descent may be remembered but the distinctive behaviour associated with the identity is discontinued. To the extent that such groups retain the Pashto language, they run the risk of ridicule: they are the ones scathingly referred to by Pathans as speaking but not doing Pashto, and retaining the pretence of being Pathans is not rewarded.

A few less ambitious niches are, however, found in the social system of the Indo-Pakistan area where Pathan identity can be perpetuated on a more individual basis. As money-lenders and as nightwatchmen, Pathans can defend and capitalize on their virtues as fearless, independent, and dominant persons, and in these capacities they are widely dispersed through the subcontinent.

Internally, a somewhat analogous loss of identity has traditionally taken place in the areas immediately under the control of the Afghan (Pathan) dynasty of Afghanistan, particularly in Kabul and the other urban centres. Here the proximity to the centralized authority is so great that it becomes very difficult for people of any importance to assert and exhibit the autonomy and independence that their identity and position demand. Somewhat incongruously, the elite and urban middle class in this purely Afghan kingdom have shown a strong tendency to Persianization in speech and culture, representing — I would argue — a sophisticate's escape from the impossibility of successfully consummating a Pathan identity under these circumstances. With the more recent developments of modern Afghan nationalism, this has changed and new processes have been set in motion.

I have analysed elsewhere (Barth 1956a) the ecologic factors that determine the limits of Pathan distribution to the north: the critical limits of double cropping, beyond which the surplus-demanding political structure based on men's house hospitality, as found in the northern Pathan areas, cannot be sustained. North of this very clear geographical and ethnic boundary is found a congeries of diverse tribes collectively referred to as Kohistanis. But this boundary also is not entirely impermeable to the passage of personnel: several groups and segments of Pathans are traditionally reported to have been driven out of their territories in the south and escaped to Kohistan, while one such 'group was encountered during a survey of Kohistan (Barth 1956b: 49). After residence as a compact and independent community in the area for four generations, this group was like neighbouring Kohistanis and radically unlike Pathans in economy, social organization, and style of life. It is reasonable to assume that Pashto, still used as a domestic language among them, will soon disappear, and that other Kohistani areas contain similar segments of genetically Pathan populations that have been assimilated to a Kohistani ethnic identity.

That this should be so is consistent with the dynamics of assimilation elsewhere. Pathan identity, as a style of life in Kohistan, must be compared and contrasted to the forms found in the neighbouring valleys, where a complex system of stratification constitutes a framework within which Pakhtun landlords play prominent parts as political leaders of corporate groups based on men's houses. By contrast, Kohistanis have a simple stratified system, with a majority of owner-cultivator commoners and a minority stratum of dependent serfs, plus a few Pashto-speaking craftsmen. Politically the area is highly anarchic and fragmented.

In general value orientation, Kohistanis are not unlike Pathans; and analogies to the institutional complexes I have described as fora for Pathan activity are also found. Kohistani seclusion of women is at the same time even stricter and more problematical, since women are deeply involved in farming and thus must work more in public, occasioning more demonstrative escape and avoidance behaviour. Councils are limited to instituted village councils, with men seated on benches in a square formation and grouping themselves as lineage representatives. Finally, hospitality is very limited, for economic reasons, and does not provide the basis for leadership: dependents are landless serfs who are controlled through the control of land.

In the contact situation, it is a striking fact that Kohistanis over-communicate their identity through the use of several archaic features of dress, most strikingly footwear-puttees of poorly cured hides, and long hair. Pathans find these rustic features very amusing, but at the same time recognize the qualities of independence and toughness that Kohistanis exhibit. Politically the Kohistani owner-cultivator is an autonomous equal to the Pakhtun landowner and men's house leader, though he speaks for a smaller group, often only his own person. Kohistanis and Pakhtuns are partners in the non-localized two-bloc alliance system that pervades the area.

Pathans who are driven off their lands in the lower valleys can escape subjection and menial rank by fleeing to Kohistan and conquering or buying land and supporting themselves as owner-cultivators. As such, they retain the autonomy which is so highly valued by Pathan and Kohistani alike. But in competition with Pathan leaders of men's houses, their performance in the fora of hospitality and gift-giving will be miserable — what they can offer there can be matched by the dependent menials of the richer areas. To maintain a claim to Pathan identity under these conditions is to condemn oneself to utter failure in performance, when by a change to Kohistani identity one can avoid being judged as a Pathan, and emphasize those features of one's situation and performance which are favourable. Just as Kohistanis find it to their advantage in contact with Pathans to emphasize their identity, so it is advantageous for Pathan migrants under these circumstances to embrace this identity. In the fragmented, anarchic area of Kohistan, with largely compatible basic value orientations, the impediments to such passing are low, and as a result the ethnic dichotomy corresponds closely to an ecologic and geographical division.

In the preceding pages, I have tried very briefly to sketch a picture of the Pathan ethnic group and its distribution. It is apparent that persons identifying themselves, and being identified by others, as Pathans live and persist under various forms of organization as members of societies constituted on rather different principles. Under these various conditions, it is not surprising that the style of life in Pathan communities should show considerable phenotypic variation. At the same time, the basic values and the social forms of Pathans are in a number of respects similar to those of other, neighbouring peoples. This raises the problem of just what is the nature of the categories and discontinuities that are referred to by ethnic names in this region: how are cultural differences made relevant as ethnic organization?

Superficially, it is true that ethnic groups are distinguished by a number of cultural traits which serve as diacritica, as overt signals of identity which persons will refer to as criteria of classification. These are specific items of custom, from style of dress to rules of inheritance. On the other hand, it is equally obvious that the ethnic dichotomies do not depend on these, so that the contrast between Pathan and Baluch would not be changed if Pathan women started wearing the embroidered tunic-fronts used among the Baluch. The analysis has attempted rather to uncover the essential characteristics of Pathans which, if changed, would change their ethnic categorization vis-à-vis one or several contrasting groups. This has meant giving special attention to boundaries and boundary maintenance.

The essential argument has been that people sustain their identity through public behaviour, which cannot be directly evaluated: first it must be interpreted with reference to the available ethnic alternatives. Ethnic identities function as categories of inclusion/exclusion and of interaction, about which both ego and alter must agree if their behaviour is to be meaningful. Signals and acceptance that one belongs to the Pathan category imply that one will be judged by a set of values which are characteristic or characteristically weighted. The most characteristic feature of Pathan values lies in giving primary emphasis to autonomy: in politics, in one's relations to material objects, in one's escape from influence and vulnerability through kin relations. This identity can be sustained only if it can be consummated moderately successfully: otherwise individuals will abandon it for other identities, or alter it through changing the criteria for the identity.

I have tried to show how different forms of Pathan organization represent various ways of consummating the identity under changing conditions. I have tried to show how individual boundary crossing, i.e. change of identity, takes place where the person's performance is poor and alternative identities are within reach, leaving the ethnic organization unchanged. I have also touched on the problems that arise when many persons experience the failure to excel, without having a contrastive identity within reach which could provide an alternative adjustment, and how this leads towards a change in the definition of the ethnic identity and thus in the organization of units and boundaries. To recapitulate in connection with the organization of the political sphere: the Pathan pattern of council organization allows men to adjust to group living without compromising their autonomy, and thus to realize and excel in a Pathan capacity. Under external constraints, as members of larger and discrepantly organized societies, Pathans seek other fora for consummating these capacities through bravery and independent confrontation with hostile forces as trading nomads, nightwatchmen, and money-lenders. In some situations, however, Pathans find themselves in the position of having to make accommodations that *negate* their autonomy: they become the clients of Baluch chiefs, the vassals or taxpaying, disarmed citizens of effective centralized states, the effective dependents of landowner/hosts. Where alternative identities are available which do not give the same emphasis to the valuation of autonomy, these unfortunates embrace them and 'pass', becoming Baluch, Panjabis, or Persian-speaking townsmen. In Swat and Peshawar District, where no such contrastive identity is available, defeat and shame cannot be avoided that way. But here the fact of such wholesale failure to realize political autonomy seems to be leading towards a reinterpretation of the minimal requirements for sustaining Pathan identity, and thus to a change in the organizational potential of the Pathan ethnic identity.

We are thus led into the problem of how, and under what circumstances, the characteristics associated with an ethnic identity are maintained, and when they change. The normal social processes whereby continuity is effected are the social controls that maintain status definitions in general, through public agreement and *de facto* positive and negative sanctions. But where circumstances are such that a number of persons in a status category, *in casu* Pathans, lose their characteristics and live in a style that is discrepant from that of conventional Pathans, what happens? Are they no longer Pathans by public opinion, or are these characteristics no longer to be associated with Pathan identity?

I have tried to show that in most situations it is to the advantage of the actors themselves to change their label so as to avoid the costs of failure; and so where there is an alternative identity within reach the effect is a flow of personnel from one identity to another and *no* change in the conventional characteristics of the status. In some cases this does not happen. There is the case of the Pathan serfs of some Baluch tribal sections, where the serfs sustain a claim to Pathan identity and have this confirmed by their Baluch masters. What is actually involved in this case, however, is a kind of shame identity: the Baluch patrons enjoy the triumph of having Pathan serfs, but do explain that these people were only the serfs of the formerly dominant Pathans. The masters were defeated and driven out, and these Pashto-speakers are not in fact their descendants. And the 'Pathan' serfs do not have access to Pathan fora and would not have their identity confirmed by Pathans. Thus, the identity retains its character because *many* change their ethnic label, and only *few* are in a position where they cling to it under adverse circumstances. Only where the many choose to maintain the claim despite their failure — as where no alternative identity is accessible — or where the failure is a common and not very costly one, as in the main body of the population in Peshawar district, do the basic contents or characteristics of the identity start being modified.

The traditional version of Pathan identity has thus been one on which a population could base a feasible pattern of life under certain conditions only, and the distribution of Pathans and Pathan social forms can be understood from this. The system has been most successful, and self-maintaining, under anarchic conditions in low production areas. Producing a demographic excess under these conditions, Pathans have spread outward: extending Pathan territory northwards, northeastward, and recently northwestward, while generating a large-scale population movement through a relatively stable ethnic boundary eastward and southward. Under changing conditions at present, with urbanization and new forms of administration, the total situation has changed so that one can expect a radical change both of Pathan culture and of the organizational relevance it is given.

---

[1] There are also in Baluchistan some persons who are the clients of commoners or corporate groups of commoners — these are few in numbers and socially and economically deprived.

[2] Except, that is, for some clearly discrepant groups like Saints, Mullahs, Dancers. etc. who recoil from or are excluded from these activities.

Neighbours in Laos

by Karl G. Izikowitz

Ethnography or social anthropology has hitherto aimed mainly at describing and analysing separate social systems from various aspects with a view to contributing to a general social theory. That the social systems of separate peoples should have received such concentrated attention may perhaps be due in part to the influence of the old national romantic movement, which sought to give prominence to each people's national characteristics and particular system of values. Possibly the countries tended to stress these as a means of holding their own against their neighbours. I shall not, however, go into this matter myself but leave it to be dealt with by historians of ideas.

As soon as a group wishes to improve its status and give prominence to its own way of life, it is faced with the problem of neighbourhood or — as I should like to call it — the relationship of different peoples living next to each other. One then leaves the study of the separate societies — *mono-ethnic groups,* and turns to that of neighbouring groups — *poly-ethnic groups.* In this article I shall give some views on questions connected with this and take as my starting point some comparatively meagre material from Laos, where I did short field-studies in 1936–38 and more recently in 1963–64. As my aim had not been to study these questions, this paper can so far only be a sketch or outline.

Indo-China is very definitely a poly-ethnic society and some very fine studies of it have already been made by E. R. Leach (1954), who deals with conditions in Highland Burma. He has later also published an article 'The Frontiers of Burma' (Leach 1960) which, however, deals chiefly with the differences between the mountain and the valley tribes. Drawing mostly from Burmese material he shows the different structures characteristic of these two different societies, and the connection between them and Indian and Chinese systems.

However, in the following I shall deal chiefly with the *contact* between the tribes in Laos and my reflections will therefore be more in line with those in Leach's book *The Political Systems of Highland Burma.*

Adaptation to neighbouring peoples, who often have entirely different ways of life, social structures, and cultures, has always been a great problem which we often see in history. In our day, however, these problems have greatly increased as a result of the influence of Western civilization on the traditional poly-ethnic societies through colonization, industrialization etc.. New relationships and new centres have been created giving rise in many cases to difficult conflicts. In many places they have also produced strong nationalistic movements which in due course, by means of schools and other media, have led to assimilation and uniformity.

'One nation, one race, one people, one culture', etc. has been more than just a slogan in nationalistic propaganda. In this struggle, minorities have often got the worst of it and, where not assimilated or eradicated, have been forced into opposition and stronger unity. Various ideologies have, of course, been used in the struggles. Philosophers and politicians have tried to solve the problems of such contesting neighbours, but the results have perhaps not always been very successful. For my part I presume that it is important to examine the situation as it appears and occurs in reality, and I think anthropologists could contribute much of value. It is not only a question of analysing the conditions and the situation in the neighbourhood but also of trying to evolve certain principles of more or less general character which could be of help in dealing with such problems.

With decolonization these poly-ethnic problems have become burning ones as a large proportion of the new states is composed of a mosaic of different tribes. Not having had so many of these problems we lack experience in the West. European countries are well on the way to being unified. They usually have a common language, common customs, etc.. In some non-European areas such uniformity can also be found, probably because the assimilation processes have already taken place. One needs only study a map of the earth's peoples to see large uniform areas, e.g. in Asia, and compare these with the areas in Southern Asia, Africa, and South America.

It is all a question of adapting oneself to one's neighbours, and of how this is accomplished. In many poly-ethnic communities, however, the various groups live apart and contact is either non-existent or limited to a minimum. Maybe one meets at markets but hardly more. But markets are neutral zones and when these become permanent, as in the case of towns, mining communities, industrial areas, plantations, etc. they become central areas and strong contacts are established there, whereas contacts are often only slight between the various tribes living out in the country. Contact is not always sought; some avoid it (a kind of political-ethnic avoidance). Tibet and Nepal are examples of this, as Bhutan also is still. It is particularly true of Burma today. Its frontiers, as we know, are closed.

What interests me here, however, are the kinds of contact which create interdependence between different groups. This causes concentration of large groupings of peoples whose relationships — be they positive or negative — form systems which generate dominant actions. These sometimes remain even when the systems change.

Laos is a very sparsely populated country (about 4 persons per sq. km) with difficult terrain, most of it mountainous. The Mekong, which flows through the length of it, is navigable by canoes for most of its course. The tributaries which flow down from the mountains are only navigable at their mouths. The country's network of roads is very underdeveloped and the few relatively new roads for motorized traffic are hardly usable except in the dry seasons. There are a few cross-country caravan paths intended for pack-horses. Within the territory of each tribe there are acceptable paths but between tribal territories these are often overgrown or almost non-existent. Large uninhabited stretches of wilderness separate one tribe from the next. The rivers and the few caravan trails were the most important means of communication before colonization; and only those who could navigate the dangerous rapids in their canoes controlled the lines of communications.

The differences between the various ethnic groups are considerable. The various mountain tribes are divided into many different language groups. Even where there are similarities in the way of life and the structure of the ethnic groups, differences exist. Most of them make their livelihood from swidden agriculture, their main produce being glutinous rice. The Mon-Klhmer-speaking peoples, the first to populate the area, are fairly permanently settled (contrary to what is often described in the French literature) which, in part may be related to the fact that there is no particular shortage of land.

The more recent immigrants from Southern China and Tonkin, the Meo- and Yao-speaking tribes, seem to be slowly spreading. Their

cash-crop is poppies from which they extract opium, the trade in which
is of great importance.

The distribution of the ethnic groups is layered. The Meo tribe
lives highest in the mountains, as do certain other tribes. Halfway
down the mountain sides and below on the plains live some farmers
practising swidden agriculture.

The valleys and river plains, where wet rice can be cultivated, are
the home of the Thai tribes. Some of them, particularly the northern
groups, have very advanced irrigation. The Thai tribes have inhabited
South China and the northern parts of Indo-China for a long time.
When Kublai Khan invaded Indo-China in 1353 the Thai tribes
acquired political power over large parts of this territory and began
to settle there and assimilate other tribes. The Thai are organized in
a state headed by an aristocracy and form a contrast to the segmented
highlanders who, in Laos, do not seem politically to have passed the
village stage. The village chiefs usually act as ritual leaders presiding
over the village council.

Thus in the Thai districts there are states and the population is
somewhat denser. The Thai tribes in Thailand and Laos are Buddhists,
whereas the rest of the Thai people, especially those in Tonkin, are not.
Upon the latter the Chinese influence has been stronger and they
have constantly been under pressure from the Chinese. The Vietnamese
have been the most influenced by the Chinese. Thai expansion has
continued right into the twentieth century, partly as a result of Chinese
pressure. During the eighteenth and nineteenth centuries a number of
Thai communities left their home districts and emigrated south; some
even moved down to the Malay Peninsula. The Mekong valley is full
of different types of Thai tribes. Some of them are very conscious of
their origin and of the fact that they differ from the Siamese and the
Lao.

Even if the Thai tribes settle in areas where they can cultivate wet
rice, a strategic trading position is of importance to them. The Lü,
a Thai tribe living mostly on the Chinese frontiers bordering on Laos
and Burma, controlled not long ago a state called Sippsong Panna.
Several villages emigrated from Sippsong Panna at the end of the
nineteenth century and settled down at points along a caravan trail
which goes from China through Laos down to north eastern Siam. It
was along this path that opium was transported and the location of the
new Lü villages was partly determined by their participation in opium
smuggling. They were a link in the chain between certain mountain

tribes, Chinese and many other members of the big international confederacy.

The Lao and other Thai controlled the trade on the Mekong. The points where each tributary from the mountains flowed into the Mekong were therefore naturally of strategic importance, and it is there we find the big Lao villages. Their names all begin with Pak which means mouth of a river. The locality was chosen to provide trade facilities with mountain tribes. Local products were collected in these villages and then sent on along the Mekong by raft and canoe. The produce of the mountain tribes consisted of shellac, cane, wax, Spanish pepper, rice, cardamom, etc. In exchange they received foresters' knives and other iron implements. They also bought pots, Lao cloth, etc.. They could only make few of these wares themselves.

These dominant Thai tribes had a very condescending attitude towards the mountain tribes. They were called *Kha* = slave, servant, and before the colonization had to pay taxes to the Lao in the form of produce and services. Those living near the Lao centres were often quite poor. Outside the Thai controlled area one finds, as Leach (1960:64) also did in Burma, the large wealthy mountain villages. Contempt for the mountain tribes is still widespread and in the political situation of today this causes quite a lot of trouble.

There is usually no intermarriage between Thai and Kha, but there are exceptions. When new Thai villages were being built along the lower parts of tributaries, the Thai men first settled at such trading stations. They took, and I have seen examples of this, wives from among the local Lamet women. Their children were Thai, and when Lao families moved in, these places became genuine Thai villages.

In certain parts such mixed marriages have had ritual significance. I have heard of a newly immigrated Thai chief in Southern Laos who gave his daughter in marriage to a Kha chief so that the latter in return should use his expertise to perform the rites for *phi muong*, i.e. the earth's or area's spirit. At the royal court in Luangphrabang there is also a custom that a Khmu chief (Khmu = a Kha tribe) should conduct the Lao king to his throne on certain occasions.

The Thai who settled down among the original inhabitants and came to dominate them were probably a small group. Gradually they managed to assimilate the earlier inhabitants. The Thai families then became an upper class and the Thai-ized inhabitants a lower class. This is particularly noticeable among the black Thai in Tonkin. One notices the difference between the two groups racially too. Leach considers that as far as Burma is concerned there are no racial differences. But I can hardly believe that this is always the case.

A Sek village (the Sek, who speak an archaic Thai language, probably came to Southern Laos very early) which I visited in 1964 was divided in two by a deep ravine. One half was inhabited by Seks and a few Lao families, the other by completely Thai-ized So (a Kha tribe), who also organized the rites for the earth spirit. Although they had the same culture as the Sek, the real Sek looked down upon them so much that they did not like my visiting the other half of their village. They held them in great contempt and marriages did not occur between members of the different village halves. Here, too, one could clearly distinguish differences in their appearances.

Intermarriage is also rare between mountain tribes. I found an exception to this in the Lamet villages in Northern Laos, where I stayed before the War, and where there had been several intermarriages with the Khmu. Both these mountain tribes considered themselves to be closely related and aboriginal in the area.

Intermarriage between different Thai tribes seems to be easier, particularly between villages close to each other. This probably has some connection with the fact that the youngest daughter usually remains in the home with her parents. She later inherits the house and what land has not been divided among her elder brothers and sisters. So when she gets married she stays at home to look after the old people. It is then usually the custom for a boy from another Thai tribe in the neighbourhood to marry her. In a future article I hope to give some statistics to demonstrate this assertion.

The difference between mountain and valley dwellers is thus considerable and is stressed by all those who have written about these parts. In this case the governing Thai tribes lord it over the subjugated Kha. The difference in status is very distinct. And it is this difference which is so marked in the present-day political division of Laos between the valley and the mountain tribes. One of its results is also that the sons of noble and influential Laos get the best jobs, whereas educated mountain tribesmen sometimes flee to Pathet Lao, i.e. the East block on the other side of the 'bamboo curtain'.

The Thai tribes and mountain tribes have up till now been in contact with each other and are still partly so, but the relationship of Laos to North Vietnam is changing this. Laos is of strategic importance to North Vietnam. Prince Soupannivong of Laos, who is related to the royal family in Lungphrabang, probably seeks to be a charismatic leader among the mountain tribes and uses them for his own strategy. Strife and quarrels about succession are, as Leach points out, a common story in the Thai area (Leach 1960:57). The power of the princes depends on the charisma they can create.

On the Vietnamese side of the Annamite mountain chain conditions are quite different but have not yet been examined. The Vietnamese can hardly have had the same contact as the Lao with the mountain tribes. They have mostly been tied by their cultivation technique: elevation irrigation. The tribes on that side of the mountains have therefore been rather independent. The Vietnamese have hardly showed any desire to settle down in the fruitful mountain valleys. During the war with the French, which ended with the battle at Dien-bien-phu and the Geneva settlement in 1954, some of the mountain Thai, the Tho, helped Viet-Minh, after their nobles had fled over to the French. During the war with the Americans the mountain tribes have also helped FNL and the North Vietnamese. These latter have, as a matter of fact, little experience of jungle and mountain terrain. The South Vietnamese have looked down upon the mountain tribes, whereas the Viet-Minh spread propaganda among them in their own language.

The difference between the relationships Thai/mountain tribes and Viet/mountain tribes is probably quite considerable. The Thai tribes and mountain tribes had more contact with each other than with the Vietnamese. I shall now attempt to explain this interdependence from a more general point of view.

To understand the poly-ethnic relationships existing between neighbouring tribes in Laos, it is necessary to make a few comparisons. I shall here limit myself to a few aspects only, and I wish my treatment of these to be considered tentative.

As far as I can see, the boundaries which separate different neighbouring ethnic groups are made apparent by the social and cultural differences between them. These differences seem to belong mainly to three categories.

1. Differences in techniques of expression, whether it be in language, ritual actions, gestures, etiquette, or customs. Here one should not overlook such important matters as, for example, customary diet.

2. Value systems, which are probably a product of the world view and the social structure. These are intimately connected with techniques of expression.

3. Self-identification. Whether they themselves consider that they

belong to the group, at least in some respects, and whether this is accepted by the members of the group. One should not forget the negative side of this attitude, i.e. that one does not consider oneself to belong to the neighbouring group. This may be important in cases where identification with one's own group is not particularly strong. Identification can change and one can consider that one belongs to one's own group only in certain situations, whereas in others one may be on the way to identifying oneself with another group.

I should like to call all these three categories *introspective,* i.e. they are directed towards the group of identification. Within it one has a social position and a certain rank.

Different conditions, however, exist for the *outward-looking* categories, which describe relationships between the different groups. Partly these may be dependent on the difference between the *introspective* traits of each of the two groups which somehow affect the relations between them. I shall not, however, analyse this here. It is a matter for later elucidation. Instead I shall turn to two categories particularly apparent in poly-ethnic relationships.

1. Identification is important, but it is of a different kind from the one previously mentioned. It is not a question of identification with one's own group but of outside evaluation of the group and whether this evaluation will be accepted. In a poly-ethnic society, I should imagine, there is often some sort of classification system based on estimates about the characteristics of different tribes. Perhaps this is true mostly within hierarchical societies where the opinions of the leading group are decisive? By means of such classification each tribe or ethnic group acquires a social position and, possibly, defined roles and special status.

2. Relations between the ethnic groups must be expressed in some forms of interaction if, that is, the different neighbours have any contact with each other. As I shall now show in an example taken from Laos, it is not a question of one sort of action but of several kinds often on different levels.

Interaction then depends on the nature of the relations, the accepted evaluation of the different ethnic groups etc., and can lead to war, rebellion, persecution, flight, the imitation of customs, peaceful trade, and many other types of action.

However, these relations between neighbours depend on their contacts and on whether the two societies are democratic or whether at least one has an autocratic system, i.e. whether it is a meeting between hierarchical or non-hierarchical societies. The forms of interaction then depend on these two forms of society, the differences reminding us a little of those between two of the more usual types of political structure.

That the meeting-places or contact zones between the ethnic groups play an important part here is rather obvious. Ecology is an important factor, as I have shown in my examples from Laos and from Leach's Highland Burma. In Laos these points of contact are often situated along lines of communication, rivers and caravan routes. It cases where these meeting-places are located on ecologically strategic sites they may be fairly stable.

There is also the question of how often these meeting-places are used. Have they permanent inhabitants or not? In Laos the Thai and mountain tribes only meet on a few rare occasions during the year to exchange wares. In other parts of the world there are permanent markets or at least regularly occurring ones. In the countries where there are states, as, for example, in Laos, small market towns often grow up where the administration is centred. One finds the more important Buddhist temples and monasteries there too and these places often attract craftsmen and trade.

In many of the countries studied by anthropologists there were no towns in the traditional community. They first came with colonization or as a result of Western influence. In modern Africa, for example, Southall (1961) distinguishes between two types of towns of this kind, and it is the ones beside plantations and mining communities which attract working-power from many different directions. Thus the towns become important poly-ethnical centres, where industries and administration create new social classes which are quite different from those in the villages. Here identification changes too. In everyday situations one might identify oneself with a certain class instead of one's own tribe. Identification changes according to one's work and the education one has received.

With these general assumptions and principles as a starting-point, one can find various combinations and types which I shall not, however, attempt to systematize here. I shall only give a few examples which may give some idea of the mobile system to be found in poly-ethnical Laos.

It is clear that in Laos there is something I should like to call a segmentary relationship. As I have already said, the Lamet and the Khmu tribes are on good terms with each other and think of each other as 'brothers', whereas there is strong opposition between them and the autocratic Thai tribes, who form another solidary unit. An exception to this are the Thai relations with the very independent tribes of Man (Yao) and Meo, which immigrated from China comparatively late. They are often literate, in contrast to the usually entirely illiterate Mon-Khmer-speaking tribes.

I should think similar situations are to be found in many parts of the world. To name but one example from Algeria (Bourdieu 1958) the relations between Berbers and Arabs there are often strained, but during the Algerian war they united aginst the common enemy. When peace returned the enmity between them flamed up anew.

Many neighbouring tribes are often entirely dependent on products from each other, making an exchange of wares and services necessary. Here, too, Algeria can provide us with an example and this complementation between nomads and farmers is probably to be found over large parts of the Orient. Even if there is enmity between the parties, they must maintain a minimum of reciprocity.

In many parts, markets are important centres for contact between different tribes, particularly when these markets are regularly in operation and are firmly established. In connection with India's first election after her independence in 1952, I noticed that election propaganda was spread in weekly markets. Up on the Koraput plateau in the state of Orissa these market places were the meeting points for all the different neighbouring tribes as well as for the Hindu customers for their products.

In the cases where some of the tribes have a hierarchical organization, something halfway between a democratic and an autocratic community is sometimes formed. Here I am thinking mainly of the extremely interesting conditions which exist among the Kachin in Burma and also of the similar oscillation between these forms of community to be found among a number of tribes in the mountains of Burma. This mixed form, halfway between the aristocratically organized Shan tribes and the democratic Kachin, Leach calls *gumsa*, a Kachin community of autocratic type but relatively unstable. It soon disintegrates and returns to *gumlao*, the name for the democratic type, only to be transformed again on some later occasion back to *gumsa*. Leach considers that *gumsa* is an imitation of and influenced by the Shan system. *Gumlao* is also unstable due to the *mayu-dama* system, whereby one obtains a different status according to whether one is a bride-taker or a bride-giver. The latter has the higher position. Thus it is a question of oscillating between one extreme and the other for the Kachin, whose already unstable *gumlao* system is strengthened by the influence from the Shan model to become *gumsa*. I do not think I need relate more from this classic work, which is probably known to most anthropologists (Leach 1954).

I have not come upon anything similar among the mountain tribes in Laos. Maybe this has to do with the lack of real chieftainship among the Mon-Khmer-speaking population. The only thing I have been able to observe is perhaps a tendency in that direction among the Lamet tribe, something which appeared with the change brought about by the labour immigration to Thailand and the introduction of money.

Gluckman has a somewhat similar example from the Zulus. Here we have three groups: the whites and the Africans, who are divided into two groups, on one hand the Christians and the native officials and on the other the non-Christians. The middle group composed of the Christians and officials are dependent on the whites. They can, however, never enter the closed circle of the whites and are at the same time drawn back by their brothers in order to build a national African union to fight against the whites. This middle group then oscillates between the whites and the non-Christian Africans (Gluckman 1958).

I do not think it would be difficult to find more examples of such middle groups, particularly in contact zones between Western societies and the traditional ones.

It is not unusual to find in several societies a system of classification whereby all kinds of groups including the ethnic ones are fitted into a hierarchy. The most well-known is probably the Indian caste system, which is applied all over India and even to such groups which are not actually Hindu. Such hierarchical relations, in their turn, generate certain typical actions. Hypergamy and dowries are part of all this and in connection with these institutions there are several financial transactions, such as the money-lending system and trade in gold and precious stones, which have played an important part in Indian society. Much of this is connected with the attempts constantly being made to improve one's social status, either in order to enter a caste, if one is an outcast, or to climb up on to a higher rung in the Indian hierarchy.

I should, however, presume that this is not only true of the quite special Indian situation but of all societies where the different groups are arranged in a hierarchy. The relationship between the aristocratic Thai tribes in Laos and their neighbours, the mountain tribes, is undoubtedly a hierarchy of this kind. Often the hierarchical system of closed groups is confused with the caste system. Differences such as those between the literate and the illiterate, as in the case of Laos, can then be of importance. The language and religion of the leading group is then forced upon its subordinates and Leach points out how quickly the Kachin tribes with their different languages learn the Thai language and adapt themselves to the Shan (Leach 1954: 239 et seq.).

Many poly-ethnic relationships depend on the existence of a centralized state authority. The towns and administration centres spread propaganda for the language and culture of the leading group. For hierarchical as well as non-hierarchical societies such central places as towns play quite a special part in the re-grouping and possible fusing together of the different ethnical groups, as I have already pointed out.

The poly-ethnic relationships in Laos are definitely hierarchical but the different groups here have not gone together to form a unit. It is still a very loose system, where one party, the Thai tribe, tries to dominate the other which it superciliously calls *Kha*. The latter wish to maintain their independence, quite an easy matter, at they can with little difficulty retire to some distant place in the mountains. There is no problem about land in this thinly populated country. In most places one can find a hill-slope suitable for swidden cultivation.

To sum up, the aristocratic Thai try to dominate the democratic mountain tribes, who simply avoid them and keep away from them as much as possible. No integration has been possible in the state of Laos and in the situation at present this division is emphasized since most hill tribes are separated from the plain dwellers by the 'bamboo curtain'. This separation of valley tribes from hill tribes is now a fact. An exception is, however, provided by immigrants from China some of whom have left the east side and settled down in the government's area. It would be interesting to know how many of these people now live west of the 'bamboo curtain'.

The Lao domination of the mountain tribes certainly dates back a long time. Before the war the Lao only managed to control the tribes living near the towns and other administrative centres. Thus the Khmu tribes around Luangphrabang have been subjugated for a long time but there were rebellions even before colonization, and several of these tribes were made slaves after they were defeated. Slavery was, however, abolished by the French in 1884 (Reinach 1911).

But the mountain tribes beyond the control of the Thai remained free. Contact with them in the form of direct visits or in the few markets in the towns through Thai merchants was peaceful. There have been marriages between the two tribes but these have certainly been very rare. Trade has indeed been the most important connection, especially as the mountain tribes have been dependent on supplies of iron wares, salt and other Thai products. Thus these relations have been of quite a different quality than the above-mentioned domination.

As the mountain tribesmen usually need money for paying the bride-price and capital for buying the valuable objects which belong to the ancestor cult and which give prestige in their own society, it has been customary for the young men to leave home to find work or to enrol as soldiers in the service of some Thai prince. The latter is the case of the *Khuen* tribe, a Khmu tribe in the province of Namntha, who used to be soldiers of the prince of Nan (Thailand). Labour could be found in the teak forest and plantations in Thailand.

The Thai tribes, however, aim at something quite different. Either they want to acquire prestige by giving presents to the Buddhist temples or by turning to politics and with the help their followers attain a position of power. Examples of this are easy to find. All the political coups which have occurred in that country since the last world war are attributable to such activity! Even if the migration or expansion of Thai groups to other parts of Indo-China has often occurred because of Chinese pressure in earlier times, it was led by men who showed charismatic qualities and acquired a following (Leach 1960:57, Izikowitz 1963).

The boundaries between the two ethnic groups are formed chiefly by differing political structures and differing aims. The ecological adaptation has probably not been so important since both groups can live side by side exploiting the same niches. Neither can the language differences be of importance since most of the mountain tribes can speak a Thai language as well as their own.

The various types of poly-ethnic relations should be considered as *social states* — i.e. parts of a social change which is taking place. Relations can in certain cases change very rapidly, particularly poly-ethnic relations of a segmentary type, where friendship and enmity alternate. They can also do so in societies with a system like that of the Kachin tribe, where there is constant oscillation between two extremes. Where there are hierarchical societies with domination relationships, attempts at assimilation occur, which lead in their turn to avoidance, flight, or rebellion.

In a state like Laos with a developed system for propaganda via schools, the Buddhist organization, etc., the poly-ethnic society may gradually turn into a mono-ethnic one in times of peace. The present-day nationalistic propaganda in many of the newly created states which were earlier colonial countries seems really to be an action towards changing the country into a national unit and obliterating the great ethnic differences. In Laos, for example, all people are called Lao but it is really only the Thai tribes who have so far showed a tendency to merge.

Industrialization will no doubt lead to a general uniformity as far as the ethnic groups are concerned. But it is a long and painful process. Instead of identifying oneself with a tribe as before, one is on the way to being assimilated into a group, where what counts is achieved status and not ascribed status.

In any case, one must examine the state in all poly-ethnic societies with special reference, among other things, to the kinds of strategy used by the different groups, whether they be ethnic units or newly-formed groups with a system grounded on education. In all such states various forms of myth-creation and propaganda appear, as well as multiple action forms, which have long interested historians. Anthro-pologists must, however, go further into these things and see which of all the relations and actions produced by poly-ethnic societies have general validity. This would certainly also be of importance to the peace research of our time. After all the whole earth is a segmentary society.

Bibliography

Aarseth, B. 1967. Status og fremtidsperspektiver i reindriften. *Sameliv: Samisk Selskaps Årbok.* Oslo.

Aguirre Beltrán, A. 1953. *Formas de gobierno indígena.* México.

Arensberg, C. M. 1963. The Old World Peoples: The Place of European Cultures in World Ethnography. *Anthropological Quarterly,* Vol. 36.

Barth, F. 1955. The Social Organization of a Pariah Group in Norway. *Norveg 5.*

Barth, F. 1956a. Ecologic Relationships of Ethnic Groups in Swat, North Pakistan. *American Anthropologist,* Vol. 5.

Barth, F. 1956b. *Indus and Swat Kohistan — an Ethnographic Survey.* Studies Honouring the Centennial of Universitetets Etnografiske Museum, 1857–1957, Vol. II. Oslo.

Barth, F. 1959. *Political Leadership among the Swat Pathans.* London School of Economics Monographs on Social Anthropology, No. 19. London.

Barth, F. 1964a. Ethnic Processes on the Pathan-Baluch Boundary. In G. Redard, ed.: *Indo-Iranica.* Wiesbaden.

Barth, F. 1964b. Competition and Symbiosis in North East Baluchistan. *Folk,* Vol. 6. No. 1.

Barth, F. 1964c. The Fur of the Jebel Marra. 'Outline of Society' for Department of Anthropology, University of Khartoum. Mimeo.

Barth, F. 1966. *Models of Social Organization.* Royal Anthropological Institute of Great Britain and Ireland, Occasional Papers, No. 23.

Barth, F. 1967a. Economic Spheres in Darfur. In R. Firth, ed.: *Themes in Economic Anthropology.* London.

Barth, F. 1967b. Human Resources: social and cultural features of the Jebel Marra Project Area. Department of Social Anthropology, University of Bergen. Mimeo.

Barth, F. 1968. On the Study of Social Change (Plenary Address to the American Anthropological Association Meeting, 1966). *American Anthropologist*, Vol. 70.

Blom, F. 1956. Vida precortesiana del indio chiapaneco de hoy. In *Estudios Antropológicos publicados en homenaje al doctor Manuel Gamio*. México D.F.

Blom, F. & La Farge, O. 1927. *Tribes and Temples*. Louisiana.

Blom, J. P. & Gumperz J. J. 1968. Some Social Determinants of Verbal Behaviour. In J. J. Gumperz & Dell Hymes, ed.: *Directions in Sociolinguistics*. California.

Bogoras, W. 1904—9. *The Chuckchee*. Anthropological Memoirs, American Museum of Natural History, Vol. II. New York.

Bohannan, P. 1963. *Social Anthropology*. New York.

Bourdien, P. 1958. Sociologie de l'Algérie. In *Que sais-je?* No. 802. Paris.

Cancian, F. 1965. *Economics and Prestige in a Maya Community*. Stanford, California.

Caroe, O. 1962. *The Pathans 550 B.C.—A.D. 1957*. London.

Colby, B. N. & van den Berghe, P. L. 1961. Ethnic Relations in Southeastern Mexico. *American Anthropologist*, Vol. 63.

Cunnison, I. 1966. *Baggara Arabs: Power and the Lineage in a Sudanese Nomad Tribe*. Oxford.

Dahl, H. 1957. *Språkpolitikk og skolestell i Finnmark 1814–1905*. Oslo.

Eidheim, H. 1963. Entrepreneurship in Politics. In F. Barth, ed.: *The Role of the Entrepreneur in Social Change in Northern Norway*. Årbok for Universitetet i Bergen, Humanistisk Serie, No. 3.

Eidheim, H. 1966. Lappish Guest Relationships under Conditions of Cultural Change. *American Anthropologist*, Vol. 68.

Eidheim, H. 1968. The Lappish Movement — an Innovative Political Process. In M. Swartz, ed.: *Local-level Politics*. Chicago.

El Hadi El Nagar & Taha Baashar. 1962. A Psycho-Medical Aspect of Nomadism in the Sudan. In *The Effect of Nomadism on the Economic and Social Development of the People of the Sudan*. Philosophical Society of the Sudan. Proceedings of the Tenth Annual Conference. Khartoum.

Falkenberg, J. 1964. Samer og fastboende i Røros-traktene. *Norveg* 11.

Ferdinand, K. 1962. Nomadic Expansion and Commerce in Central Afghanistan — a sketch of some modern trends. *Folk*, Vol. 4.

Ferdinand, K. 1967. Ættelinjestabilitet Blandt Nomader i Øst-Af-

ghanistan. Paper submitted in advance for participants in the
Wenner-Gren Symposium on 'Ethnic Groups', Bergen Feb. 23rd to
26th 1967.

Furnivall, J. S. 1944. *Netherlands India: A study of Plural Economy.*
Cambridge.

Furnivall, J. S. 1948. *Colonial Policy and Practice.* London.

Garvin P. L. 1958. Comment on the Concept of Ethnic Groups as
Related to Whole Societies, by Herbert H. Vreeland. In W. Austrin,
ed.: *Report of the Ninth Annual Round Table Meeting in Linguistics
and Language Studies.* Washington.

Gjessing, G. 1954. *Changing Lapps: A Study in Culture Relations in
Northernmost Norway.* London School of Economics Monographs
on Social Anthropology, No. 13. London.

Gluckman, M. 1958. *An Analysis of the Social Situation in Modern
Zululand.* Rhodes-Livingstone Papers, No. 28. Manchester.

Goffman, E. 1959. *The Presentation of Self in Everyday Life.* New
York.

Goffman, E. 1963. *Stigma: Notes on the Management of Spoiled
Identity.* New Jersey.

Greenberg, J. H. 1966. *Languages of Africa.* Bloomington.

Guiteras Holmes, C. 1946. Informe de Cancuc. Microfilm Collection
of Manuscripts on Middle American Cultural Anthropology, No. 8,
University of Chicago Library.

Gumperz, J. J. 1958. Dialect Differences and Social Stratification in
a North Indian Village. *American Anthropologist,* Vol. 60.

Haaland, G. 1968. Nomadization as an Economic Career among
Sedentaries in the Sudanic Savannah Belt. Department of Social
Anthropology, University of Bergen. Mimeo.

Izikowitz, K. G. 1963. Expansion. *Folk,* Vol. 5.

Kandre, P. 1967a. Autonomy and Integration of Social Systems: The
Iu Mien (Yao) Mountain Population and their Neighbours. In P.
Kunstadter, ed.: *Southeast Asian Tribes, Minorities, and Nations.*
Princeton.

Kandre, P. 1967b. Om etnisitet hos Iu Mien-Yao i Thailand, Laos och
Burma. Paper submitted in advance for participants at the Wenner-
Gren Symposium on 'Ethnic Groups', Bergen Feb. 23rd to 26th 1967.

Kirke- og undervisningsdepartementet, ed. 1959. *Innstilling fra komi-
téen til å utrede samespørsmål.* Oslo.

Kleivan, H. 1967. Grønlendere og andre dansker: Identitetsunder-
strekning og politisk integrasjon. Paper submitted in advance for

participants in the Wenner-Gren Symposium on 'Ethnic Groups', Bergen Feb. 23rd to 26th 1967.

Knutsson, K. E. 1967. *Authority and Change: A Study of the Kallu Institutions among the Macha Galla of Ethiopia.* Etnologiska Studier 29, Etnografiska Museet, Gothenburg.

Kroeber, A. L. 1939. *Cultural and Natural Areas of Native North America.* Berkeley, California.

Leach, E. R. 1954. *Political Systems of Highland Burma: A Study of Kachin Social Structure.* London.

Leach, E. R. 1960. The Frontiers of Burma. *Comparative Studies in Societies and History,* Vol. III.

Leach, E. R. 1967. Caste, Class and Slavery — the Taxonomic Problem. In A. de Reuck & J. Knight, eds.: *Caste and Race: Comparative Approaches.* London.

Mitchell, J. C. 1956. *The Kalela Dance: Aspects of Social Relationships among Urban Africans in N. Rhodesia.* The Rhodes-Livingstone Papers, No. 27. Manchester.

Moerman, M. 1965. Who are the Lue: Ethnic Identification in a Complex Civilization. *American Anthropologist,* Vol. 67.

Nadel, S. F. 1947. *The Nuba.* Oxford.

Narroll, R. 1964. Ethnic Unit Classification. *Current Anthropology,* Vol. 5, No. 4.

Paine, R. 1965. *Coast Lapp Society II: A study of Economic Development and Social Values.* Tromsø Museums Skrifter, Vol. IV. Oslo.

Pehrson, R. 1966. *The Social Organization of the Marri Baluch* (compiled and analysed from his notes by F. Barth). Viking Fund Publications in Anthropology No. 43. Chicago.

Pineda, V. 1888. *Historia de las sublevaciones indigenas habidas en el Estado de Chiapas.* San Cristóbal Las Casas, Chiapas.

Pitt-Rivers, J. & McQuown, N. A. 1964. Social Cultural and Linguistic Changes in the Highland of Chiapas. Department of Anthropology University of Chicago. Mimeo.

Pozas Arciniega, R. 1948. *Juan Pérez Jolote: Biografía de un Tzotzil.* Acta Anthropologica, Vol. III, No. 3.

Pozas Arciniega, R. 1959. *Chamula: Un pueblo indio de los altos de Chiapas.* Memorias del Instituto Nacional Indigenista, Vol. III, México D.F.

Redfield, R. & Villa Rojas, A. 1939. *Notes on the Ethnography of the Tzeltal Communities of Chiapas.* Carnegie Institution of Washington, Publication No. 509, Contribution 28.

Reinach, L. 1911. *Le Laos*. 2 vols. (posthumous edition compiled by P. Chemin-Duponts). Paris.

Sahlins, M. D. 1958. *Social Stratification in Polynesia*. The American Ethnological Society. Washington.

Siverts, H. 1960. Political Organization in a Tzeltal Community in Chiapas, Mexico. *Alpha Kappa Deltan*, Vol. 30, No. 1.

Siverts, H. 1964. On Politics and Leadership in Highland Chiapas. In E. Z. Vogt & A. Ruz Lhuillier, eds.: *Desarrollo Cultural de los Mayas*. Universidad Nacional Autónoma de México.

Siverts, H. 1965a. *Oxchujk': En Mayastamme i Mexico*. Oslo.

Siverts, H. 1965b. Some Economic Implications of Plural Society in Highland Chiapas. *Folk*, Vol. 7.

Siverts, H. 1965c. The 'Cacique' of K'ankujk': A Study of Leadership and Social Change in Highland Chiapas, Mexico. *Estudios de Cultura Maya*, Vol. V. Mexico D.F.

Sommerfelt, A. 1967. Inter-etniske relasjoner i Toro. Paper submitted in advance for participants in the Wenner-Gren Symposium on 'Ethnic Groups', Bergen Feb. 23rd to 26th 1967.

Southall, A. 1961. *Social Change in Modern Africa*. London.

Sundt, E. 1850–65. *Beretning om Fante- eller Landstrygerfolket i Norge*. Christiania.

Villa Rojas, A. 1942–44. Notas sobre la etnografía de los indios tzeltales de Oxchuc. Microfilm Colection of Mss. on Middle American Cultural Anthropology, No. 7. University of Chicago Library.

Villa Rojas, A. 1947. Kinship and Nagualism in a Tzeltal Community, Southeastern Mexico. *American Anthropologist*, Vol. 49.

Vogt, E. Z. ed. 1966. *Los zinacantecos: Un pueblo tzotzil de los altos de Chiapas*. Instituto Nacional Indigenista. Colleción de anthropología social, Vol. 7. Mexico D.F.

Vorren, Ø., ed. 1960. *Norway North of 65*. Tromsø Museums Skrifter, Vol. VIII. Oslo.

Ward, B. 1965. Varieties of the Conscious Model: The Fishermen of South China. In *The Relevance of Models for Social Anthropology*. A.S.A. Monographs 1. London.

The Symposium
and Its Participants

This collection of essays presents the results of a symposium in which a small group of Scandinavian social anthropologists cooperated in a joint effort to further the analysis of ethnic groups. The symposium meetings, supported by a grant-in-aid from the Wenner-Gren Foundation for Anthropological Research, were held at the University of Bergen, 23rd to 26th February 1967. The participants were Klaus Ferdinand, Aarhus; Karl Gustav Izikowitz and Karl Eric Knutsson, Gothenburg; Peter Kandre, Stockholm; Axel Sommerfelt, Harald Eidheim and Helge Kleivan, Oslo; and Henning Siverts, Jan-Petter Blom, Gunnar Haaland, and Fredrik Barth, Bergen. A brief statement of problems and a sketch of analytical concepts by Barth was circulated with the original invitation. Participants then prepared their essays in advance of the meeting, and these were circulated. After the meetings it was decided to publish the results in one book, and each participant was invited to revise and rewrite his essays as he saw fit. Seven complied with this wish, and Barth wrote the general introduction, basing it on his original points and on the results of the discussion, drawing freely on the essays in their original or revised forms. The result is thus in a real sense a joint product from all the participants which, we feel, illustrates the application of some common analytical viewpoints to different sides of the problems of poly-ethnic organization in different ethnographic areas. As host to the symposium I wish to thank all the participants for their contribution to its success, and to express our joint appreciation to the Wenner-Gren Foundation for making our work possible.